GW00854472

10 Storm: Der Schimmelreiter

Critical Guides to German Texts

EDITED BY MARTIN SWALES

STORM

Der Schimmelreiter

Alfred D. White

Senior Lecturer in German
University of Wales College of Cardiff

Grant & Cutler Ltd
1988

© Grant & Cutler Ltd
1988
ISBN 0 7293 0300 4

I.S.B.N. 84-599-2545-5

DEPÓSITO LEGAL: V. 2.674 - 1988

Printed in Spain by
Artes Gráficas Soler, S.A., Valencia
for
GRANT & CUTLER LTD
55-57, GREAT MARLBOROUGH STREET, LONDON W1V 2AY

to my wife Diana

and my children Christian, Andreas, Gideon and Abigail

Contents

Contents

Prefatory Note

The page numbers in brackets in this text refer to pages of *Der Schimmelreiter* in the Reclam edition mentioned in the first item of the Select Bibliography. The 1985 printing, in which the text runs from p.3 to p.146, is used. Other references, indicated in brackets by italicised figures, are to the numbered items in the Select Bibliography.

My thanks are due to my colleague Dr David Jackson for his unstinting help and willingness to discuss Storm problems, though this does not mean that he agrees with all my conclusions.

Introduction

As soon as Theodor Storm had finished writing *Der Schimmelreiter*, he read it aloud in his family circle. A hundred years ago, in an old-fashioned small-town or village household like that of the Storms, the telling of stories — fact or fiction, written down or committed to memory — was a vital part of family life. Rarely could they visit the theatre; entertainment outside the home mainly meant visits to a few like-minded families, or readings and concerts arranged by a small group of the more cultured townspeople. In such an atmosphere, imaginative response to literature was nurtured. Without images provided ready-made by theatre, cinema or television, intuitive understanding and visual imagination were used freely. Storm was a committed story-teller who never wrote a play, never relied on actors and sets and props to flesh out his words. He attends solely to providing food for the mind of the reader or listener. The limitations of narrative, which can work only with words, are a threefold challenge to him: to his craftsmanship in describing exactly those things which the reader must be clear about; to his skill in leaving scope for us to visualise people and circumstances; and to his inspiration in choosing subjects which repay the investment of interpretative effort. Storm's response to these aesthetic challenges will be considered in the following chapters, as will some of the other elements of his literary greatness: how he takes up the life of a small area he knew well and gives it general relevance, how he uses historical sources, how he builds up images of people and social interactions, how he uses eerie and paranormal phenomena, how he structures and arranges the data of the story.

The literary work must contribute to and enlarge the reader's interpretation of the world. We shall see that this story is about reason and religion, progress and reaction, technology and nature, individual and mass, self-interest and common good, man and woman; in each of these areas Storm has things to say which we should be foolish not to listen to today, for none of these dichotomies has disappeared in the intervening hundred years. But one should take it first as 'a good read', a gripping story. The apparition of the white horse rider at the outset poses a puzzle not finally explained until the very end (and even then not unambiguously solved); Hauke's doings and the building of the dyke provide constant conflict and sustain our interest in the outcome; forebodings and hints of the supernatural are skilfully strewn to fascinate us. If we have not first enjoyed the story and let ourselves be carried away by it, deeper analysis of it will bear little fruit.

In my treatment of the story, duplication of elements has been avoided as far as possible. Thus the question of Trin' Jans's cat, which belongs in at least three chapters, is to be found only in the chapter on Trin'; Wienke, similarly, only under 'Family'. And no coherent character-study of Hauke will be found, as his character is determined by all the other aspects — how he behaves in social and family relations, how he is linked to the horse, and so on. The reader is asked to excuse the one-sidedness and incompleteness of individual chapters brought about by this procedure, in the interest of freeing space for other interesting elements.

1. Storm's Life

Hans Theodor Woldsen Storm (14.9.1817 Husum - 4.7.1888 Hademarschen) was the eldest of thirteen children. His father, a lawyer, came of an old family from inland Holstein — the eldest sons had been called Hans for generations —, his mother of a Friesian patrician family, the Woldsens (Storm was given their family name to prevent it dying out). Their home was Husum, a small port that had seen better days, on the flat west coast of Schleswig. Storm grew up in a traditional well-to-do atmosphere but without religion, and he never felt a need for faith; by family tradition, upbringing and character he belonged to a conservative, even parochial, variant of the democratic liberalism frequent in the professional middle classes of mid-European states at the time. As a boy, not spoilt by too visible shows of affection from his parents, he found himself activities outside the home, hearing and telling traditional local tales, soaking up the landscape. Only after going to the *Gymnasium* at Lübeck at the age of 18 did he discover modern literature: Heine and Eichendorff. He also met Emanuel Geibel, a poet slightly older than himself, later the darling of cultured Germany for his formally lovely, but empty verses. After studying law at the universities of Kiel and Berlin, Storm took up legal practice in Husum in 1843. His first mature poems date from this time, but by the late forties he was devoting more time to writing short stories. For the rest of his life literary work occupied him a great deal and meant a welcome addition to his often meagre income.

He fell in love with a cousin, Constanze Esmarch, to whom he wrote some impressive poems; they married in 1846. A stormy period followed, marked by his passion for Dorothea Jensen, whom he was eventually to marry after Constanze's death. Only after Dorothea left Husum did Storm find emotional equilibrium; in time he grew to love Constanze passionately and depend on her for moral support — and comments on his works before they went to publishers. He was a difficult, wayward husband, who wanted a wife educated enough to converse with him, old-fashioned enough to obey him, and tolerant enough to put up with him. A possessive father, if unfashionably unauthoritarian, he founded much of his self-esteem on his paternal qualities; in later years he was full of self-pity when he thought he had failed as a father — there were seven children of his first marriage. Sickly or hypochondriacal, humourless, vain, insecure, he felt impotent in the face of circumstances and was deeply alone.

Husum lay in the Duchy of Schleswig, one of the two German-speaking provinces of Denmark. In the 1840s the Schleswig-Holstein question was becoming one of the main problems of nineteenth-century power politics. In the complicated Europe of the post-Napoleonic era, the King of Denmark belonged to the *Deutscher Bund* in his capacity as Duke of Holstein, but no other; and he was concerned to bind both Schleswig and Holstein more closely to Denmark. But in that time of nationalist strivings the population of both duchies was more inclined firstly to express discontent with Danish rule, secondly to stress that Schleswig and Holstein were inseparable, and thirdly to look beyond this to some concept of a German nation, more tightly organised than the *Deutscher Bund*, and incorporating both duchies. The most extreme defined this Germany, even then, in terms all too familiar in our century: of race, *Volkstum* and opposition to a foreign tyranny (*14*, pp.170ff.). It is perhaps fair to say that most people, Storm too, were local patriots for Schleswig-Holstein independence, with phases of seeing a future German nation as the best frame for this. Storm came into conflict with the authorities because he supported independence, writing political poems during the war of 1848-50 (in which the rebels in the duchies were at first supported by Prussia) and signing a protest against the results of the 1849 truce between Denmark and Prussia. In 1850 Prussia finally abandoned the cause of the duchies, Denmark giving worthless guarantees to Prussia and Austria to respect the special situation of Schleswig-Holstein.

Forbidden to practise law because of his continual protests at Danish rule, Storm unwillingly left Husum in 1853 and took a post in the Prussian judiciary, though he hated its pedantry, rigid ways and overwork. In Berlin he moved in literary circles. After a training period at Potsdam he was transferred to Heiligenstadt, far from Berlin, in 1856, as *Amtsrichter*. All this time his father had to supply money to eke out the poor Prussian pay. In 1863 the Schleswig-Holstein question again blew up; Danish attempts to bind Schleswig more closely to the Danish crown were countered by the emergence of a rival claimant to the two duchies, whom Austria and Prussia supported in order to establish a joint suzerainty of their own in Schleswig-Holstein. In 1864, though the fate of his home was not settled, Storm returned to Husum, having been elected *Landvogt* (town clerk, magistrate and head of constabulary); in this demanding and well-paid post he found himself increasingly caught between the traditions and rights of the people and the ever heavier hand of his *bête noire*, the Prussian bureaucracy — for the Prussians treated Schleswig more like conquered territory than like an independent duchy. Though disillusioned at the prospect of spending his life under the *Junker*-dominated state, he could not face a second exile. He found solace in his family, but in 1865 Constanze died. A year later, after some time spent travelling to escape memories of her, he heeded the promptings of his old passion and gave his children a good stepmother by marrying Dorothea; there was one child of this second marriage.

Prussia picked a quarrel with Austria, and completed the *de facto* annexation of Schleswig and Holstein in 1867. The conversion to the Prussian system was marked by a cut in Storm's pay; with the following separation of executive and judicial powers, he became an *Amtsrichter* again, relinquishing his administrative duties. At this time the illness and heavy drinking of his eldest son Hans started to worry him. He had a growing correspondence with other authors such as Keller, Heyse and Fontane, literary critics and historians, and younger admirers; he wrote hard (and earned more in royalties, to his relief, as his work grew a little better known), and ran the Husum *Musikverein* which he had founded. After his mother's death he took early retirement in 1880 and went to live inland, in a villa he had had built at Hademarschen in Holstein, so as to work, and enjoy his garden, undisturbed. It was here that during the writing of *Der Schimmelreiter* Storm felt the onset of the illness which was to kill him (see Chapter 4). Here too he died in 1888, but his body was taken for burial — without a priest, as he had wished — to the Woldsen family vault in Husum.

2. Storm's Works up to 1885

The beginning of Storm's literary career coincides with the emergence of Realism as a trend in German literature, seen in the later stories of the Romantic, Ludwig Tieck, and the country tales of Adalbert Stifter and Berthold Auerbach. Storm started with poems, written mainly between 1844 and 1853; in 1847 he began to write stories — idylls, *Märchen*, anecdotes, sad minor-key depictions of wasted or blighted lives. His lyrical, delicate story of memory, *Immensee* (1850), was a major event in the history of literary realism. He continues to exploit this vein in many stories, such as the quietly presented yet stark tragedies of *Auf dem Staatshof* (1856-58) and *In Sankt Jürgen* (1867). The atmosphere, landscape and ways of his home area are dominant; in clinging largely to rural settings Storm is a typical German realist, a contrast with authors such as Dickens or Balzac who grasped the modern themes and settings offered by large cities. Germany was lacking in such opportunities, so that German realism sometimes seems cosy, backward and provincial until, much later, Theodor Fontane, a friend of Storm's, starts to depict the metropolis of Berlin.

Storm develops his powers of description early, but only slowly learns to deal with character, plot and social circumstances clearly and directly; this too is typical of German authors of the time, who often seem to believe that atmosphere is more important than action. His early heroes tend to be weak men, given to having unhappy love-affairs and living gloomily ever after when they fail (thus *Immensee*); a vague fatalism discourages any strenuous attempts to forge one's own destiny, or to examine one's life from a moral viewpoint. In most of his stories, narrow personal relationships, pessimistically viewed, are central. Misunderstanding and ambiguity are often shown as spoiling the fine web of human affection. The plot is often slight. Storm long cultivates an indirect mode of narration — some stories consist of a series of static descriptions, and the reader must reconstruct the events in between; many have a frame in which we meet a narrator who admits to not knowing all the facts of the story he is to tell; or situations are described as if by an outsider who does not know even the names of the people involved. There seems to be no objective underlying reality; the characters, and the author, move on thin ice over a void.

Draußen im Heidedorf (1872), with its realistic portrayal of a village community steeped in superstition, is an indication that Storm's artistic attitudes are gradually changing. He embraces the idea of the omniscient narrator and insists less on the uncertainties, ambiguities and nuances of life. The active hero trying to take control of his fate begins to appear, even if the kind of activity that came into fashion in the *Gründerjahre* of the new Germany seems uncongenial to Storm and he often flees the Bismarckian present, the era of 'Might is right', for historical settings. (The way he thrusts the plots back into history, and his fondness for complex frames, also suggest that he needs to hold at arm's length some deep unacknowledged personal emotion.) In consequence his plots grow more complex, the structure firmer, the descriptive passages more closely linked to the theme.

But at the same time Storm, like other writers at this time, shows a new willingness to face down-to-earth realities. Stories such as *Carsten Curator* (1877) oppose traditional ways to the new materialism and keen business sense of the epoch. He starts to show life's hard edges, cruelties, even vulgarities; he points out the fateful gaps between social classes, the ineluctability of tragedy. His settings are still largely the village and small-town ones he knows best. The only route to universal significance for men such as Storm, Gottfried Keller, Wilhelm Raabe and the rest, who were at home in the conservative atmosphere of the small states of nineteenth-century central Europe, starts from something closely defined, intimate, even provincial. But concentration on a closed society and use of historical settings do not prevent the writer hinting at the social and ethical problems of a community in change, as *Der Schimmelreiter* shows.

Storm was not fond of exploring new subjects and approaches opened up by the economic and political progress of Germany and the growing role of the middle class; he remained a pragmatic writer, little influenced by developments he did not see at first hand, by intellectual fashion or by abstract theory; his political views never developed beyond the staid small-scale democratic ideals of 1848 and the hatred of Prussia and the German Empire for betraying them; but he did observe social realities, the rural proletariat for instance, more closely as time went on. Acquaintance with Darwin's theories of evolution, and their interpretation by Social Darwinists as legitimising a struggle of all against all among mankind, gave a pessimistic intellectual framework to some of his later work. Themes of generation conflict, alcoholism and involuntary guilt found in the late stories certainly reflect his own experience, especially his relationship with his alcoholic son Hans; but they also anticipate the new literary movement of Naturalism, rising in Germany by the time of Storm's death (Gerhart Hauptmann: *Bahnwärter Thiel*, 1888), which makes more systematic use of new scientific theories, realism in speech, and concentration on the lower classes.

The dead hand of the nobility is a constant theme of Storm's historical stories: he bitterly opposed the aristocratic hegemony in Prussian society, though he personally found colleagues with a *von* to their name (von Wussow in Heiligenstadt, von Reventlow in Husum) congenial and cultured. *Aquis submersus* (1876) forms a microcosm of his obsessions: the strongest statement of his opposition to the *Junker* class, together with a rounded portrayal of an artist, a strongly defined conflict, an unhappy love and an element of personal guilt, all set in a past era that yet has analogies with the present. The clergy is attacked here and in *Renate* (1878), a tale of superstition in the seventeenth century. The unresolved tension of unexplained mysteries and naturalistic tendencies in *Renate*, criticised by Keller (letter of 13 August 1878: 7, p.40), prefigures *Der Schimmelreiter*.

3. *The Writing of* Der Schimmelreiter

In 1885 Storm commenced research for this story, whose theme he had 'Jahre lang herumgetragen' (to Erich Schmidt, 16 February 1888, *10*, II, p.146), but he repeatedly put off its writing in favour of other, shorter works. The integration of the real elements of history and dyke-building with the fictional, even mythical, parts could not be rushed. 'Jetzt aber rührt sich ein alter mächtiger Deichsagenstoff in mir, und da werde ich die Augen offen halten; aber es gilt vorher noch viele Studien! Die Sache wird ein paar Jahrhunderte [zu]rück liegen' (3 February 1885, *10*, II, p.107). Nine months later Storm says he is leaving it till the new year (18 November 1885, *10*, II, p.119). He mentions his 'große Lust' to write the 'Deichnovelle', but also doubts — 'wenn ich es nur noch werde bewältigen können' (4 December 1885, *6*, III, p.123). Or he complains 'Ich begänne so gern die beabsichtigte Deich- und Sturmnovelle, aber sie müßte gut werden, da sie so heimathlich ist; doch ich kann nicht; auch fehlt mir so viel im Material, was ich zur Zeit nicht schaffen kann. Die kurze Zeit und die sich darin noch dazu verkürzende Kraft, das drückt mich mitunter' (28 March 1886, *10*, II, pp.124f.). Later, despite distractions and physical weakness, he reports having done various studies and started on the story (8 July 1886, *10*, II, p.129). Then his doubts recur: 'In Arbeit ferner: "Der Schimmelreiter", eine Deichgeschichte; ein böser Block, da es gilt eine Deichgespenstsage auf die vier Beine einer Novelle zu stellen, ohne den Charakter des Unheimlichen zu verwischen.' (29 August 1886, *6*, III, p.140).

In October he contracted pleurisy. In December he heard of his son Hans's death; this set back his recovery. In March 1887 he was able to start writing *Ein Bekenntnis*, and in May had taken up *Der Schimmelreiter* again (25 May 1887, *6*, III, p.151); but when in the same month he asked his doctor for the truth about his illness and was told he had cancer of the stomach, he grew so depressed as to endanger the work's completion. So his brother and another doctor gave a fake second opinion that he merely had a distended aorta. This succeeded in giving him the will to continue writing. Distractions such as the public celebration of his seventieth birthday slowed work down; chronic stomach pains did not help as he faced the writing of the second half late in 1887. Half consciously he probably still knew he was dying and hurried to finish the story. Not for nothing does he make Antje Wohlers die of cancer — not a typical marsh disease as he claims (p.52; see also *14*, p.13). By autumn 'Mein vielgenannter "Schimmelreiter" ist bis S.92 der Reinschrift gediehen, und Sonntag will ich nach Heide um mit meinem Deich-sachverständigen Freunde Bau-Insp. Eckermann ein Nöthiges weiter zu besprechen. Aus einem Jungen ist Hauke Haien nun auf dieser 92. Seite zum Deichgrafen geworden; nun bedarf es der Kunst, ihn aus einem Deichgrafen zu einem Nachtgespenst zu machen' (20 October 1887, *6*, III, p.161).

In that December Storm was still learning about dykes, though the manuscript had grown to 127 pages of fair copy and 30 in draft (3 December 1887, *9*, p.177). 'Im Januar werde ich wohl mit dem "Schimmelreiter" fertig, dem Größten [i.e. longest], was ich bisher schrieb. Ich denke, wenn auch nicht das Ganze, so wird Dich einzelnes interessiren' (18 December 1887, *6*, III, p.162). On a visit to Husum after Christmas, and on his return to Hademarschen, he worked at the manuscript every morning. On 9 February 1888 he completed it and read it to his family; yet again he wrote gloomily: 'Ich hätte ihn wohl vor 10 Jahren schreiben sollen; jetzt ist denn geworden, was rebus sic stantibus werden konnte.' (11 February 1888, *6*, III, p.166). In the following weeks he made corrections and additions and corrected proofs; the story appeared in the *Deutsche Rundschau* for April and May 1888, and the positive reaction of his expert friends Schmidt and Heyse surprised and gratified him (17 May 1888, *6*, III, p.173). But he did not live to see *Der Schimmelreiter* published in book form.

4. The Sea, the Dyke and Hauke: Storm's Sources

Storm was deeply attached to his home town by the sea, Husum, and its environs. The sea as a route to foreign parts meant little to him, but the town, the shore, the mudflats, the fens, the heath, a great deal; many of his poems that are staples of German verse anthologies, such as *Die Stadt* or *Abseits*, were inspired by these settings, their changing moods, sunny, wild, melancholy. He lovingly studied local history and folklore from boyhood on. *Der Schimmelreiter* reflects all this as does the poem *Meeresstrand*:

> Ans Haff nun fliegt die Möwe,
> Und Dämmrung bricht herein;
> Über die feuchten Watten
> Spiegelt der Abendschein.
>
> Graues Geflügel huschet
> Neben dem Wasser her;
> Wie Träume liegen die Inseln
> Im Nebel auf dem Meer.
>
> Ich höre des gärenden Schlammes
> Geheimnisvollen Ton,
> Einsames Vogelrufen —
> So war es immer schon.
>
> Noch einmal schauert leise
> Und schweiget dann der Wind;
> Vernehmlich werden die Stimmen,
> Die über der Tiefe sind. (*4*, I, pp.112f.)

His constant view of the sea as a threat — 'die große, wüste, menschenfeindliche Nordsee' (31 October 1842, *8*, p.28) — is rooted in the local experience of disaster. A great flood in 1825 showed him that the sea can suddenly conquer the fruitful land and men must work continually to recover and protect their achievements. There were many floods before and have been since — up to 1976 — in the history of North Friesia (the west coast of Schleswig-Holstein): that of 1362, for example, swept away the legendary town of Rungholt; that of 1634 drowned 6,000 people; that of 1756 Storm uses as the occasion of Hauke's death. A chronicle he used says of it:

> Der Wind wehte an demselben Tage erstlich aus dem Westen, nachhero drehete selbiger sich nach Nord-Westen, und fing an dergestalt heftig zu werden, daß auch die aller älteste Leute dergleichen Sturm-Wind gehört zu haben, sich nicht entsinnen können.
> So heftig dieser Sturm war, so heftig fing das Wasser an zu steigen. Die Wuht desselben war unbeschreiblich.
> Die Hattstetter-Marsch brach durch und bekam eine Wehle von 7 Ruhten breit und 16 Ruhten tief...[1]

In 1885 Storm approached Christian Hinrich Eckermann, an expert on dyking, land reclamation and dyke history, for a plan of the Nordstrand and Husum area as it was before 1634. By using actual locations the realist Storm ensures contact with everyday reality for a work whose symbolism and supernatural elements could easily have led to pseudo-romantic, vague lyricism and unreality. Though Storm does not follow his models slavishly, the Hattstedt area seems to be the basis for Hauke's home village.

The new fen corresponds to the *Hattstedter Neuer Koog*, an area of about five square kilometres, the one thousand *Demath* of the story; Jevershallig to the old Jakobshallig, now also part of a reclaimed fen; the *Priel* to the old *Königstief*; the town to Husum. The inner frame could be set at the inn of Sterdebüll,

[1] *Sammlung einiger Husumischer Nachrichten* (Flensburg 1750ff.), facsimile in *3*, p.136.

now called *Schimmelreiter-Krug*, a long, low, thatched, typical
Friesian building; near it the crater made by the 1756 flood is
now a reed-grown depression. But this is at the south end of the
Koog, whereas the story demands the north end, away from the
town. Hattstedt church with its typical stone tower, well known
to Storm whose second marriage took place in Hattstedt, is
probably the model for the church. The Lundenberger Hof,
family home of a friend of Storm's, *Deichgraf* Johann Iwersen-
Schmidt, buried in Hattstedt in 1875, gives a basis for the big
farm. Storm also depicts everyday dyke maintenance and
building techniques realistically, down to the 'Frühlingsschau'
(p.33), when the state of the dykes after the winter was regularly
examined, and the 'einspännige Sturzkarren mit Gabeldeichsel'
(p.91), ancestors of the dumper truck. The mouse damage in the
old dyke is a detail from the flood of 1825 (*14*, pp.157f.).

Critics have often sought a historical model for the hero too.
The text mentions Hans Momsen of Fahretoft (1735-1811), and
uses an anecdote (the Dutch edition of Euclid) found in a
memoir of Momsen published in 1874 (*14*, p.142). Hauke like
Momsen is self-taught, cool about religion, uninterested in
farming, opposed to superstition (*14*, p.149); but Momsen had
little interest in dykes. Hans Iwert Schmidt, father of Storm's
Deichgraf friend, lost his life in a ditch near his house whilst
checking the state of the dyke riding a white horse; his long
cloak, blown around his head by the wind, made the horse shy
(*14*, p.165). But nothing else about him suggests Hauke. More
relevant is Martin Andresen, *Deichgraf* of Pellworm in the early
nineteenth century, who left embittered after long struggles
against the farmers' resistance to his dyke works. The identity of
the originator of the gently sloping dyke profile which Storm
credits to Hauke was long lost in the fog of time and confused
traditions; Storm cannot have been clear on this. In fact a
Dutchman, Johann Claussen Rollwagen, appointed *General-
deichgraf* in 1609, introduced the wheelbarrow and the
improved dyke structure to the area. Popular tradition confused
this man of integrity and talent with another Dutchman, Johann
Claussen Coott, a speculator who built shoddy dykes (*14*, pp.91-
100). Jean Henri Desmercières, who was responsible for a spurt

of reclamation in the area from 1733 on and reintroduced the shallow profile, was a hard-headed Copenhagen bank director; he took an informed interest in the execution of his works, but without 'Haukean' obsessiveness.

Individual features of such men, the technical gift of a Momsen, the entrepreneurial drive of a Desmercières and so on, are united by Storm in one man, a 'Superdeichgraf' (*19*, p.21). Like Momsen he is of the area, but unlike that popular figure, around whom anecdotes gathered, he is treated as an outsider: someone like Desmercières, whom local people prefer to forget, or the Claussens. Storm knowingly diverges from history, disregards the involvement of outsiders and posits that the local community had in Hauke's time, as in long-past centuries, the resources, organisation and motive to undertake major dyking work itself. On the historical basis that for about a thousand years the North Friesians, without claiming independence of their successive overlords, had resisted the strong feudalising tendencies otherwise apparent in Schleswig and maintained a peculiar way of life with remnants of a tribal, pre-feudal structure, Storm shows a self-contained community. But in fact in the sixteenth century the Dukes of Gottorp as territorial rulers had laid claim to ownership of the foreshore (*14*, p.85), so the local community would not have benefited from dyking as Storm describes. Successive rulers issued licences to individuals to dyke and take over parcels of the foreshore. The local people were uneasy at no longer being in charge: they had only to suffer the influx of rowdy workers from inland, rent and farm the newly-won land and pay taxes on it.

A *Deichgraf* single-handedly conceiving and pushing through a scheme of land reclamation with local resources was impossible. Only in showing that officialdom (the *Oberdeichgraf*) counts for all in dyke matters, the views of the natives for nothing (p.88), does Storm approach historical truth (*14*, pp.86ff.). Even the affluent Desmercières had to sell a large estate inland to finance his dyking works (*14*, p.137); a Hauke and his fellow-villagers could never have built a dyke on the basis of the rough profit-and-loss calculation Storm presents (p.70). After 1803 a reorganisation of dyke administration again led to greater local involvement; important works were carried out by Christian Friedrich Salchow, local *Deichinspektor* from 1819 to his death in 1843. He leased a house in Husum from Storm's father, and is probably the model for Sternow in Storm's *Der Herr Etatsrat*, whose professional eminence contrasts with an objectionable private personality. In general, local people took little initiative in dyke building until after Storm's death (*24*, pp.74-81, 114-16; *14*, pp.89-101).

Disregarding all outer influences, all population movements and mixings, Storm shows the Friesian standing alone through the centuries in the battle with the sea, a tragic conflict full of opportunities to show a local characteristic, stubbornness. In thus tendentiously celebrating the Friesian in Hauke Storm, unwittingly, provides material for racist nationalism (*14*, pp.175f.). On the other hand, if the Danes are excluded, so too are the Prussians denied a role in the world of the story, 'des Friesen imaginäres Vaterland' (*14*, p.177).

Fictional dykegraves are possible influences on the story too. In the outer frame Storm suggests a source in a magazine, mentioning his own great-grandmother's house as the place where he read it. His statement is misleading: the old lady died in 1829, but the source is *Lesefrüchte vom Felde der neuesten Literatur des In- und Auslandes* published by J.J.C. Pappe in Hamburg, Volume 2 (1838). Here we find a story of some 900 words, *Der gespenstige Reiter*, subtitled *Ein Reiseabenteuer* (reprinted in full in *4*, IV, pp.655-57; *40*, pp.61-64), borrowed from a Danzig periodical, the *Danziger Dampfboot* of 14 April 1838. It begins: 'Es war in den ersten Tagen des Monates April im Jahre 1829 — so erzählte mir mein Freund —, als Geschäfte von Wichtigkeit mein persönliches Erscheinen in Marienburg erforderlich machten...' (*4*, IV, p.655). The setting is the River Vistula; to get from Danzig (today Gdansk) to Marienburg (Malbork) the narrator, prevented from using the Dirschau ferry by bad weather and high water carrying ice, has to ride along the river bank through the stormy night to the Güttland ferry. He hears a wildly galloping horse first behind, then in front of him, which shocks both him and his horse; then the invisible animal returns past him, now visible as 'die anscheinende Gestalt eines weißen Pferdes, mit einem schwarzen, menschenähnlichen Gebilde darauf sitzend' (*4*, IV, p.656). Shaking in every limb he takes refuge in a hut used by the men who have to protect the dykes against ice damage. He does not tell his story, afraid of being teased.

But something rushes past the window and the men spring up hastily: 'Es muß irgendwo große Gefahr sein, denn der Reiter auf dem Schimmel läßt sich sehen' (*4*, IV, p.657). The last quarter of the story gives the explanation the narrator is then offered for the apparition: 'ein entschlossener, einsichtsvoller und allgemein beliebter Mann' (*4*, IV, p.657), a *Deichgeschworener* there, on such a day as this when an ice blockage was causing high water, rode to and fro on a white horse giving instructions to avert disaster; but in vain: 'das Wasser fand durch den Damm einen Durchweg, und schrecklich war die Verheerung, die es anrichtete' (*4*, IV, p.657). Seeing the breach, the supervisor accused himself of not attending enough to that point, and spurred his horse on into the water. Since then horse and rider are seen whenever there is danger. The next day the narrator completes his journey.

Storm transfers the tale to his home area. In 1842 when planning to compile a collection of local legends he wrote to his friend and collaborator Theodor Mommsen:

> Ich hab Ihnen früher erzählt, wie es Abends an unsern Deichen und am Strande ist;...immer, wenn ich Abends und allein dagewesen, hat es in mir zu diesen unheimlichen Gestalten angesetzt, die in den mir über Alles unheimlichen Deich- und Strandsagen ihre volle Verkörperung erhalten. Der Schimmelreiter, so sehr er auch als Deichsage seinem ganzen Charakter nach hierher paßt, gehört leider nicht unserm Vaterlande; auch habe ich das Wochenblatt, worin er abgedruckt war, noch nicht gefunden. (*8*, pp.48f.)

Later he mentions 'eine gewaltige Deichsage, von der ich als Knabe las' (to his daughter Lisbeth, 20 February 1885, quoted in *40*, p.40) and 'die, ich glaube, ostfriesische Sage vom "Schimmelreiter", die...ich in meinem achten oder neunten

Jahr, Gott weiß wo, las, und nicht habe wiederfinden
können'(to Frau Eckermann, 10 February 1885, quoted in *40*,
p.40). The story is coming nearer home! A divergent account is
in *Lena Wies*, 1873, boyhood reminiscences of a woman who
used to tell Storm stories in Low German, among them perhaps
'die Sage von dem gespenstischen Schimmelreiter..., der bei
Sturmfluten nachts auf den Deichen gesehen wird und, wenn ein
Unglück bevorsteht, mit seiner Mähre sich in den Bruch
hinabstürzt...' (*4*, IV, p.405). But Storm remembers her as a
reader of magazines, so the story need not be a local traditional
one. Lena, incidentally, like Wienke in our story, had a dog
called Perle (*4*, IV, p.401). The evidence for this or related tales
on the North Friesian coast is slight. In Storm and Mommsen's
collection of stories, as eventually published (after ill-feeling
between the collaborators) by the third partner, Karl
Müllenhoff, a *Strandvogt* of Sylt wanders on the beach to save
shipwrecked mariners in atonement for a past crime; and a
dykegrave on the Elbe estuary is forced into the waves while
inspecting the dykes, and afterwards seen nightly on his white
horse. To sum up, we need not believe that Storm got the story
from anywhere but the *Lesefrüchte*; later in his life he may well
have confused the experience of reading it at the age of twenty-
one with reading or hearing cognate tales in his boyhood.

5. Hauke Haien and his World

The world of *Der Schimmelreiter* is highly self-contained, and is populated, except for the pastor and the schoolmaster, by members of a single class, farmers; the royal authorities are distant, scarcely interfering except to collect taxes or give the new fen the name of a princess (which does not stick); when it is a matter of appointing a new *Deichgraf*, the nominally responsible *Oberdeichgraf* merely confirms a choice which arises naturally from among the community. The people pay ground dues, but buy and sell land without reference to a ground landlord; the community has no local *Junker* to oppress it. A *Deichgraf* can command service only for the maintenance of the dykes, and cannot pass on his position automatically by heredity, though here this has happened for three generations, and, just as occurs with the nobility in Storm's view, degeneration has set in. Social status is determined by area of land owned, ambition shown by acquiring land. The landless are employed contractually (*Groß-* and *Kleinknechte*) or casually (*Tagelöhner*); large landowners have a special position in the dyke hierarchy as 'die größten Interessenten'. But individuals move across categories. Hauke, son of a small landowner, is a casual, then a contractual, employee without feeling demeaned, then rises above his original status. The landowners' hierarchy is seen in such things as the choice of a team for *Eisboseln*: the social status of the would-be players counts more than skill in the game. Ole Peters, a *Großknecht* though a day-labourer's son, tries to use his influence to exclude Hauke, but the counter-arguments that he is a landowner's son and *Deichgraf* in all but name win the day.

Into this simple world Storm puts a complex hero. The name Hauke is an invented Friesian version of Hugo. Physically a fine and characteristic specimen, the character earned the enthusiasm of nationalistic and Nordic-minded critics with his blond hair, grey eyes, thin frame and long Friesian face (p.63). Storm insists on his local attributes as a member of 'dem tüchtigen und besonders nach der friesischen Seite sehr intelligenten Schlag Menschen hier herum' (To Heyse, 21 November 1875, *6*, I, p.100). Unlike many Storm heroes he has a good understanding with his father, a man of few words, intelligent and forward-looking. But he grows up motherless and alone; his masculine, technical, theoretical, unsensuous attitude and contemptuous disregard of the less intelligent may be at least partly attributed to this. Fascinated by his father's surveying (p.9), he early turns from general culture — primer and Bible — to Euclid, a work he always has with him to devour in meal breaks (p.11). Heredity sets him on his path — a naturalistic feature; but he goes beyond his father when he studies the Euclid with no help. To talent he adds an active element, a wish to make his mark. He soon conceives the plan of an improved dyke profile: he is on the way to a rationalistic world view. Elke complains 'Komm, sieh mich erst einmal an! Was hast du, deine Augen sehen so ins Weite?' (p.68): he sees what is distant and abstract, but may overlook the near and personal. When Tede looks ironically on his early strivings and over-confidence, perhaps he dimly realises the dangers of Hauke's attitude. A lack of interest in agriculture (p.11) betrays his narrowness.

He is familiar with sea and shore, not afraid of drowning at high tide, refusing to fear the supposed ghosts of Norwegians; self-reliance is an early achievement. He is quite willing with the aid of rationality to match himself against the elements and the uncanny. He is unable to make personal relationships; his schoolmates mean nothing to him. By aptitude, ambition and marriage Hauke will form a career for himself. He cannot gain scope to exercise his talents and bring his plan of a new dyke shape to fruition unless he has the position of *Deichgraf*, which means having more land. His aptitude comes first, his ambition afterwards. He claims power because he can use it, not because he lusts for it; one is reminded of Brecht's *Der kaukasische Kreidekreis* where Grusche claims the baby on the grounds of what she can do for it. His father early sets about increasing his holdings (p.52), though it is clear that he cannot acquire enough land to carry the office. Meanwhile Hauke follows his own way. He wants to become Tede Volkerts' farmhand and be near the mathematician Elke (p.24), but when he goes to enquire about the job he also takes the opportunity of appraising her looks (p.25); perhaps he arrives at his eventual deep love for Elke only after seeing her first as a mathematical companion and then as an heiress.

As Volkerts' hand he has a chance of overcoming in hard work the violent streak that made him kill Trin's cat, of becoming more familiar with people by participating in the work of the farm, and of working for the general good in the dyke management; but he deals with problems by trusting in, and developing, his own abilities, not by co-operation. And unfortunately working *for* the dyke expresses itself as working *against* the people who damage and neglect it. This colours his view of people, and theirs of him. They appear to him as egocentric, revolving on their own axis — symbolically — at the dance: 'die Menschen kamen ihm wie Narren vor...jeder sah nur auf seine Dirne und drehte sich mit ihr im Kreis herum' (pp.46f.). In Volkerts' house he develops his own view of the world, 'vielleicht um so mehr, je weniger ihm eine überlegene Einsicht zu Hilfe kam, und je mehr er auf seine eigene Kraft angewiesen war, mit der er sich von jeher beholfen hatte' (p.29). His employer can offer no guidance because, in contrast to the excessively rational Hauke, he is essentially animal, characterised by gluttony. On the other hand, this contrast can be seen as that of rounded life and one-sided cerebration (*18*, p.166).

Early on, the reader has little reason to suspect dangers in Hauke's character: he is a youth whose rough edges can still be smoothed down by Elke's influence. In his embarrassment when he buys a ring for her (p.49) we are clearly invited to identify with him, despite some irony of presentation. But there is a threat that his attitude to his environment will grow eccentric. With the dance it becomes apparent he is not for company; his isolation from the community is deepened on this day. Its vitality and sensual pleasures pass him by; he is afraid to dance because he might make himself and Elke ridiculous (p.48). He has the misfortune of continual strife with Ole Peters, who treats his superior intellect with the resentment and enmity of the tough but slow-witted. Hauke has no social skills, no feeling for the less advanced mentality of most people around him, no idea of man-management which might enable him to reach an accommodation with Ole. In the *Eisboseln*, a climax of their reationship, Ole tries to repress Hauke against the better interests of the team; Hauke, no better, behaves (though only when Elke comes to support him) as if with his second throw he single-handedly won the game, disregarding everyone else (p.45). Again and again he fails to foresee others' natural reactions to his behaviour, and when they turn against him, he loses control and is unreasonable to them. Later he finds it impossible to present the dyke project less abrasively, to woo general support for his way of thinking.

As his reason and reasonable self-confidence grow in the light, another side of him grows in the dark. He still feels frustrated and sees the world as a conspiracy against him; he nourishes secret ambition, hatred and mistrust (p.57). It is perhaps an immature attitude, but then he is scarcely twenty-four when made *Deichgraf*. When he weighs up the possibility of becoming *Deichgraf* he is well aware that by the 'Schärfen und Spitzen, die er der Verwaltung seines alten Dienstherrn zugesetzt hatte' (p.57) he has queered his own pitch; but this realisation does not make him conciliatory. The row of hostile faces he imagines on this occasion reappears in his mind when envious Ole half-jokingly accuses him of being *Deichgraf* through his wife: he imagines, he does not check the reality, and hears their laughter 'noch höhnischer, als es gewesen war' (p.67). Indeed, his ambition has so far been more apparent to them than his aptitude. But he takes such evidences of dislike too seriously, as insults that he cannot tolerate. The man who strives for a personal eminence knows no way but to secure his own position at whatever cost to others, facing their self-defensive opposition with a defiant demeanour. He is obsessed with the need to impose his own ideas and prove that he can, as Elke puts it, 'ein Amt regieren' (p.68).

He decides to build the dyke in the wrong frame of mind,

'under the whip of emotion' (*33*, p.766), less for personal gain, for fame, for posterity or for the community's good than to prove himself against the common view. Opposition is needed for him to give his best: at the *Eisboseln* Ole's hostile remarks draw forth Elke's intervention which gives Hauke's arm 'Stahlkraft' (p.45); and later, after Ole scorns him, Elke supports him and he gets to work on the new dyke 'als seien plötzlich die Flügel ihm gewachsen' (p.68). Hauke's final failure will be due to self-incurred isolation and enmity with society, a fault inseparable from his greatness. He sets himself against two malevolent forces, man and sea. He thinks first of the perfect dyke and its benefit to his reputation, not of the people who will have to build it. 'Certainly, he gives distinguished service to the community; but this service is only a means for him; his ends and motives are strange and dubious' (*32*, p.188). When Manners dies and Ole takes his place, no one involved in the works has a spirit of humility; hubris and superstition are pitted against each other. Hauke's pride allows him to see himself head and shoulders above all his fellow-Friesians, the dyke as his memorial.

When he broaches the question of the new dyke Elke objects that the cost will be great: Hauke counters this by referring to eventual profit. He is seen here as a hero for the entrepreneurial age of the time of writing: independent, single-minded, arrogant, ambitious, a master of useful technology, concerned to make money, neglectful of social responsibility and personal relations. He is a landowner able to extend his property, both by taking advantage of the shares in the new fen that fall to him, and by buying up the shares of others who cannot or will not contribute to the building of the dyke; he has even bought shares in the *Vorland* before having the idea of the new dyke, 'teils in dem dunklen Gefühle eines künftigen Vorteils, teils bei Vermehrung seiner Schafzucht' (p.70): Ole's accusation that he has indulged in a sort of insider trading is plausible. The progress of the community, the provision of work and prosperity for many, is inseparable from Hauke's private profit: 'denk nur um zehn Jahre weiter — dann stehen wir vor einem andern Besitz' (p.83). The profit motive, Storm shows, has existed well before his own time; it is not a product of industrialisation; there is no basic difference between a closed, traditional rural society and an open, innovative urban one. But the rural society is able to close ranks, whether — positively — to fight the threat of flooding together, as in the frame narration, or — negatively — to reject the outsider Hauke.[2]

Neither Hauke's rise in the social scale, nor his self-enrichment, are seen negatively. They are not what makes him into an unpleasant, harsh and isolated character. Storm does not see him as a boorish parvenu or moneygrubber, and does not shed doubt on the concept of progress. Hauke is, with all his faults, a true eighteenth-century progressive leader, enlightener and moderniser, heir to a tradition of geometrical learning which has been dormant for generations, attempting to make the community break out of its traditional ways, which seem lazy to him, and embark on great works for its own good. The schoolmaster narrator sees him as representative of a current of progress running down the ages: a man ahead of his time. Even before Hauke's rise there are supporters of progress, enlightened men who wisely submit to his leadership because they see his competence. They thus mediate between the asocial progressive Hauke and the more or less bigoted, superstitious, reactionary, lazy and envious majority. They may not have his driving energy but do have more sense of the community and tradition: notably Jewe Manners, in a sense Hauke's social conscience, after whose death trouble with the dyke-builders becomes unmanageable. It is a friend of his who encourages the workers to go on after the argument over the dog, something which Hauke should but cannot do, and thus pulls Hauke's chestnuts out of the fire for him, protecting him from the confrontation he has courted (p.107).

In this society, gradual change is possible, the dead hand of the gentry being absent, and the skilful or ambitious have chances to make their mark and bring about progress. Not only

[2] Harro Segeberg, 'Ferdinand Tönnies' *Gemeinschaft und Gesellschaft* und Theodor Storms Erzählwerk...', *Deutsche Vierteljahrsschrift für Literatur...*59 (1985), 474-96.

Hauke does this: Ole Peters woos his way to Jeß Harders' estate too — they are two sides of the same coin. Hauke becomes the richest man in the village without harming anyone, his dyke can be built and hold against a major flood. But Storm is equally clear about the opposing forces, as seen in the self-destructive aspects of Hauke's character and in the superstition and bigotry of the community. Thus he reflects a state of affairs that recurs throughout human society: a person of energy and intelligence lacking the tact to carry others with him in his ideas, set against a community with many positive values but unthinkingly hostile to new departures.

6. Hauke and his Family

Women play little part in the society of the story. They belong almost a priori to the less educated and thus to the superstitious and bigoted sector of the community, for example Vollina and Ann Grete; Elke is the sole exception. An heiress may be rich, as Vollina is, but on marriage she reverts to a peripheral role in the community and a subordinate one in the household. Only Trin' Jans and Elke stand apart from the patterns. They form a counterweight to Hauke in the story, standing for the chain of generations, for motherhood. Elke brings Trin' in when, a typical widow with no surviving children, she is threatened with destitution because old age and weakness reduce her earning power. As an old servant of Elke's grandfather she has a right to be looked after. The patriarchal paternalistic system shows its effectiveness; but this extension of benevolence beyond the immediate family is an exception.

Elke like Hauke grows up motherless, isolated in a male-dominated society. She is the one person with whom he can have understanding and communication. In her as in him something deeper lives, behind her 'Rätselbrauen' (p.42). The phrase 'getreue Elke' (p.143) has a fairy-tale ring; her reaction to the white horse and her fears in her fever suggest a gift of second sight. She is independent, self-confident, open, and a natural mediator, trying to smooth things over between Hauke and Ole, later between Hauke and the workers. Her talent in calculation marks her out as a natural ally — perhaps too much so, since she then cannot effectively oppose the later excesses of his ambition. With her learning and competence she has one, very understated, moment of thinking that she might be the equal of a man: when she tells the *Kleinknecht* Hauke that the *Oberdeich-graf* has in effect praised his work, he replies that she too deserves praise; she answers that when she alone helped her father there was no such praise — for he sees, more than she does, what is wrong far out on the dyke, not only in the paperwork. He disclaims any intention to usurp her place; and only 'nach kurzem Sinnen' does she reassure him that she is not offended: 'das ist ja Mannessache!' (p.36). Thus she renounces her independence. Soon afterwards her commitment to Hauke is implied by her waiting up to hear whether he is allowed to take part in *Eisboseln* (p.40).

After his father's death she rearranges his house, makes it seem bigger and lighter, imposes a feminine influence on it (p.53). Later, Tede Volkerts' death at one stroke frees the position of *Deichgraf* and makes possible Hauke's marriage to her which will give him the necessary acreage: a fortunate but not improbable set of circumstances. Because his marriage, and thus his enrichment, obviously cannot take place — because of the year's mourning — before the appointment of a new *Deichgraf*, Elke has to take the active role and reveal their engagement: 'einem rechten Manne wird auch die Frau wohl helfen dürfen!' (p.66). Tactfully she declares she will transfer her estate to him beforehand so that he is the richest man in the village (p.65). Her love and trust lead her to engineer the award of the *Deichgraf*'s post to Hauke. The alliance of his talent and her possessions is made possible by her wise handling of the situation.

All that he does, whether or not he discusses it with Elke, relies on her unquestioning support. She is not given a chance to object to his plan for the new dyke until he has fully worked it out; he does not confide in her what has troubled him — the taunt of being *Deichgraf* through her; the new plan and the work involved take him physically and mentally away from her; but she does not protest. Their very closeness casts doubt on her independent existence. She develops a surrogate pride in being the wife of the most influential man in the community, pointing out that others merely envy him:'die wären alle gern, was du bist!' (p.68). Although left too much alone and working too hard, she is happy. When she is ill Hauke, dimly realising the need for the feminine in life, and in himself, prays for her survival because he needs her. When she is told she will recover, her first concern is to assure him 'Ich bleibe bei dir!' (p.101): in a sense she is only part of him. He appeals to her 'Bleib mir treu!' (p.101), asking not for marital fidelity but for continual support. There is peace under the roof (p.111); up to a point threats such as outer enmity or Wienke's backwardness merely strengthen the family. The marriage is, if not perfect, at any rate a success in its own unsentimental terms.

When Hauke capitulates to the after-effects of marsh fever and gives up the idea of repairing the damage to the old dyke properly, he does not tell Elke of his problems, thus again injuring the ideal of openness within the family: 'ihm unbewußt war die klare Einsicht...seines Weibes ihm in seiner augenblicklichen Schwäche ein Hindernis, dem er unwillkürlich auswich' (p.126). Turning his back on her understanding and competence, he also denies himself. Once again the woman is the mirror of the man.

This self-betrayal on Hauke's part is the beginning of the end. He allows fear of another argument, and perhaps fear of jeopardising the respect he has earned by courting unpopularity, to stop his plans for altering the old dyke, something which in his obsession with the new he has so far disregarded. He shows an untypical readiness to cease striving. To show his mental turmoil Storm added at a late stage the passage from 'ein paarmal, wo er dort hätte vorüber müssen, ließ er sein schon gesatteltes Pferd wieder in den Stall zurückführen' to 'die unheimliche Stelle aufs neue zu betrachten' (p.128). Storm explained:

Wenn die Katastrophe aus der Niederlage des Deichgrafen im Kampfe der Meinungen stärker hervorgehoben würde, so würde seine Schuld wohl zu sehr zurücktreten. Bei mir ist er körperlich geschwächt, des ewigen Kampfes müde, und so läßt er einmal gehen, wofür er sonst stets im Kampf gestanden; es kommt hinzu, daß seine zweite Besichtigung bei heller Sonne die Sache weniger bedenklich erscheinen läßt. Da aber, während Zweifel und Gewissensangst ihn umtreiben, kommt das Verderben. Er trägt seine Schuld, aber eine menschlich verzeihliche...Es muß für ihn bedacht

werden: die Scheu, nach endlich vollendetem Werk den
Kampf aufs neue zu beginnen. (To Ferdinand Tönnies,
7 April 1888, *11*, II, pp.386f.)

His duel with the sea, 'unser Kampf' (p.134), takes place in
the final storm. He leaves wife and child in the house to which,
as he says, no flood has yet risen. Despite their prayers, 'der
Sturm setzte nicht mehr aus; es tönte und donnerte, als solle die
ganze Welt in ungeheuerem Hall und Schall zugrunde gehen'
(p.135). An apocalyptic 'Sündflut' (p.142) is to be unleashed.
He has given up his convictions in the face of men's opposition:
for this he finds himself guilty (p.141). The storm shows the
limits of human power and reason, the victory of 'Nacht',
'Tod', 'Nichts' (p.137): the point is reached at which Hauke has
failed. Only when the dyke is broken does he realise what he has
done. Not by accident is it a light shining across from his house
and reminding him of his wife and child which encourages him
to face the consequences of his failure to renovate the old dyke.
What he did wrong by turning away from Elke, he intends to
make good thanks to this 'Trost' (p.141). The death of his
family in the flood takes this comfort away and leads him, as the
flood itself could not, to despair: 'Das Ende!' (p.143). The
reason why Perle, Elke and Wienke leave the safety of the house
is not given. If this worries us, we may account for it by a
symbolic interpretation: that a part of Hauke, namely the
feminine side without which he is incomplete, was killed off
when he failed to take Elke into his confidence. After the breach
of the old dyke the consequences of his sin of omission have
become clear and the feminine side is missed; however much he
regrets it and now says he wants to help others, he cannot. Elke's
physical end symbolises this incapacity; it remains only for him
to take his cue from the last words of the wise woman Trin' and
sacrifice himself.

The pathetic figure of Wienke is important in several ways.
Firstly, born belatedly after nine years, she seems to reflect the
underdeveloped state of the marriage. Dyke-building serves a
desire to extend the Haien estate, and, as Elke asks earlier, for
whom does one build if not for one's children (p.83)? But this

child cannot appreciate her inheritance. Elke suffers most, remaining alone because such a child is no company; the family's situation is at its lowest ebb until Elke insists on talking about Wienke and Hauke gives her comfort: then she 'war mit ihrem Leid nicht mehr allein' (p.118). Secondly, Wienke by her helplessness calls forth unsuspected qualities in Hauke, who shows through her that he can give as well as receive love and is not a pure egotist: '...an der Wiege seines Kindes lag er abends und morgens auf den Knien, als sei dort die Stätte seines ewigen Heils' (p.102). Perhaps the adoration of his daughter is exaggerated, or, as has been said, merely a modified self-adoration; but to me it shows Hauke's humanity, at a point where Storm needs to develop this in order to counteract the effect of Hauke's elitism and his harshness to the workers, which have given colour to the accusation that he is in league with the devil. His personality splits: his family is treated well and sees the tender side, others, even household servants, are treated badly and see arrogance, which cuts him off further from the wider community.

Thirdly, Wienke's backwardness has been interpreted as a punishment for various failings of Hauke's: for his and Elke's looking forward to her father's death (p.58), for his general egoism and lovelessness, or for his neglect of Elke in favour of the dyke work. Giving his whole life to his mission, he perpetuates himself in works: the dyke lives after him. Thus he cannot perpetuate himself in the family line. Given the vague ideas of the connection of biological heredity and personal activity current at the time (Storm believed his active use of his talents had deprived his sons of vital force), this interpretation merges into a biological one: genius is not infinitely inheritable. Tede Haien jokes that 'im dritten Gliede soll der Familien-verstand ja verschleißen' (p.28), but it is no laughing matter. The family, for the conservative Storm, is a point of light, of inherited values, in a world of change and chaos, but it cannot last. The highly bred intellect of the two families, going back through three or four generations, produces an idiot child. Any family happiness is subject to decay. Storm underlines the pessimism by having the family extinguished at the end.

Fourthly, she is connected with the theme of a sacrifice to make the dyke hold. When Elke first mentions this, Hauke says 'Da ist es gut, daß wir keins [Kind] haben, sie würden es sonst noch schier von uns verlangen!' (p.72). Indeed she is claimed eventually. Finally, there is her role in the discussion of Hauke's hubris. Born in the year of the start of the dyke works (p.98), she shows by her backwardness that there are things before which even the great dyke-builder is powerless. Her belief in his omnipotence is a tragic irony. He knows he is not all-powerful. But he does believe that the concrete realisation of his thoughts, the dyke, is enough protection against the elements. Wienke's 'Kannst du nicht alles?' (p.116) and her demand for magical reassurance that the sea cannot hurt them challenge him to assume divine omnipotence; he evades her and replies 'Nicht ich kann das, Kind...aber der Deich, auf dem wir reiten, der schützt uns, und den hat dein Vater ausgedacht und bauen lassen' (p.116). He need no longer personally defy the sea as when he was young, because of the fruits of his own work. An ambiguity remains. Her relationship with him is a parody of a man-God relationship. As far as she is concerned he is omnipotent. She is affected by religion and grieves over the mermaid in Trin's story who cannot go to heaven; she dreads what she does not understand — birds, water. But in this respect she, the retarded child, is on a level with most of the population! Hauke has perhaps risen above the level of the majority of men; does he resist the temptation to set himself on the same plane as God?

7. Religion and Superstition

Storm mistrusts, but does not condemn or repudiate belief in, the paranormal. Without it, after all, his story would not exist. He wrote to Keller once 'nicht zu vergessen, daß wir hier an der Grenze Nordfrieslands, wie in Schottland, uns in der Heimat des Zweiten Gesichts befinden. Ich stehe diesen Dingen im einzelnen Falle zwar zweifelnd oder gar ungläubig, im allgemeinen dagegen sehr anheimstellend gegenüber; nicht daß ich Un- oder Übernatürliches glaubte, wohl aber, daß das Natürliche, was nicht unter die alltäglichen Wahrnehmungen fällt, bei weitem noch nicht erkannt ist' (4 August 1882, 7, p.119). Storm's daughter writes: 'Gar zu gern hätte er selbst eine wirkliche Spukgeschichte erlebt..., aber das Reich der Geister blieb ihm lebenslang verschlossen. Es herrschte derzeit in Husum, wie überall im Norden, noch mancher Aberglaube, besonders vom zweiten Gesicht wußte man viel zu erzählen.'[3] He chooses to present this story, full as it is of second sight and the inexplicable, through a rationalist narrator. He expects rational people to keep their paranormal experiences to themselves and not feed others' superstitious dread or anxiety. 'Schweig aber still davon, man darf dergleichen nicht verreden!' (p.81), says Iven to Carsten.

But not all that is irrational is harmful; the reader will decide where the dividing-line is between second sight and mere superstition. Storm's traditional symbolism with supernatural implications, such as the white horse itself, emphasises that even the supposedly rational eighteenth century can perhaps engender myths, and that there is a transcendent, timeless pattern of

[3] Gertrud Storm, *Theodor Storm: Ein Bild seines Lebens* (Berlin: Curtius, 1912-13), I, p.161.

human experience not expressible by purely rational means. To some extent he illustrates people's 'penchant to clothe their doubts and fears in supernatural beliefs',[4] but the role of the supernatural in the story can by no means be reduced to that.

Superstition is part and parcel of the ways of the village, as one would expect in an isolated area around 1750. The idea of corpses as 'Seeteufel', the whole 'Schimmel' complex, hints of Trin's witchcraft, the idea of throwing a living thing into the dyke foundations, the story of the mermaid which Hauke rebukes Trin' for spreading (pp.119f.), the phenomena on the other shore — it is not a surprising quota. Hauke stands aloof from superstition. Where he meets it he resists or refutes it and its effects. The world view that leads to it is at odds with his rationality, as with Elke's. Superstitious beliefs and magical practices are men's attempts to counter malevolent forces in nature which are beyond human control; Hauke believes in other measures to control nature. Even as a youth he confronts the eerie head on, going out on the shore attracted by 'das Grauen' (p.15) engendered by the finding of corpses, and not letting dread take over (p.16); he seems to regard the sea ('die Wasser') as a set of quasi-personal powers which he can defy: 'Ihr könnt nichts Rechtes...so wie die Menschen auch nichts können! (pp.13f.). It is perhaps the only way he can express his primary struggle to impose reason on both sea and man.

Elke's mention of a belief that something living — formerly a gipsy's child — must be thrown into the foundations of a dam (p.72) is based on Friesian (and not only Friesian) superstition. A child is said to have been buried in repair works at Mariensiel after the 1717 flood. Müllenhoff has a story of a child being bought from a gipsy woman when all efforts to fill a breach otherwise had failed. That it is the moderate Elke who mentions the superstition disposes us to take the rational side in this argument. We approve when Hauke later commands a halt to the workers' attempt to throw a dog into the works as a surrogate (pp.105f.) and rejects the old superstition as a crime or

[4] Roger Paulin, *The Brief Compass: The Nineteenth Century German Novelle* (Oxford, Clarendon Press, 1985), p.125.

blasphemy: 'Bei unserm Werke soll kein Frevel sein!' (p.106). But the superstition does have a religious core, being intended to propitiate a higher power. The anger with which Hauke summarily rejects the idea of a sacrifice shows that irrational forces of his deepest being are stirred by this threat to the idea that his planning and work alone can produce the intended effect.

The conventicle is the focus of opposition to Hauke. Ann Grete, a member of this sect, brings home the stories of occult events on the opposite shore. The weathercock blown down and a 'groß Geschmeiß vom Himmel' (p.130) — probably a swarm of insects, not unknown in August — are treated as fact by the schoolmaster. The pea-sized skulls in the pastor's washbowl (p.131) on the other hand are no doubt pure delusion; the red rain explicable by dust in the atmosphere or rain falling on red algae. Storm borrowed these phenomena from Anton Heimreich's chronicle of 1668 (quoted in *40*, pp.53f.). In the credulity of the people, whose prejudice in favour of the irrational forms their very perceptions, we meet an instance of a pervasive ambivalence. The same people who soberly do their day's work, sow and reap, baptise and bring up their children and improve their property, also see sea-devils and mermaids (*16*, p.461). North Friesian society was traditionally tolerant, not to say indifferent, in religious matters. From about 1600 various sects took refuge or arose there. The growth of the conventicle in the story and Hauke's reaction — better there than in the *Schnapskrug*! — are characteristic, if over-simplified (*14*, p.62; *24*, pp.69f.). To Storm it exemplifies mere bigotry. In it, among people who have failed in practical life and with the leadership of a foreigner, the forces of reaction gather.

Even before it, the superstitions about the white horse, and Ole's jealousy, set opinion moving against Hauke. But we should not see a simple conflict of Hauke, great and always right, against the rest, mean and wrong. A wiser Hauke would have taken the prevalence of superstition into account, or even put it to use for his plans. In a way the purchase and exclusive use of the white horse is a foolish challenge, feeding that superstition that Hauke would like to stamp out (*19*, p.82). Not sectarian misfits, but respectable workers, argue seriously with Hauke about Christianity and heathenism. They think throwing a dog into the dyke is the truly Christian way of proceeding, he calls their convictions 'Heidenlehren' (p.107). Trin', similarly, equates disbelief in mermaids with atheism; the sectarians accuse him of godlessness because he does not share their bizarre views. They say, and people listen to them, that he denies God; what he really denies is God's power to alter the laws of nature He has laid down. Storm makes Hauke's views clear. The supposedly blasphemous prayer is truly a prayer; he thinks of himself as a Christian and is not tempted to set himself up as God. Does his denial of God's omnipotence show that he himself is in the grip of hubris?

He can be bitterly sarcastic about God — 'es ist nur ein verantwortlich Amt, die Gemeinde vor unseres Herrgotts Meer zu schützen' (p.128) — but he is not godless, he has just 'sich sein eigen Christentum zurechtgerechnet' (p.98) — a telling verb: a religion for his rational, egocentric world view. His God, made in the image of the mathematician, is in charge of what men do not understand: the weather, Elke's childlessness (p.83), her recovery when given up by the doctor. Thus he only prays when all human recourse is vain, not knowing whether he prays 'aus Andacht oder...nur, um in der ungeheueren Angst sich selbst nicht zu verlieren' (p.98); and he prays selfishly, to be allowed to keep Elke because 'ich kann sie nicht entbehren' (p.99). He calls on God: 'da machen wir mit Gott den Schluß!' (p.108). At the end he asks Elke: 'bete zu Gott, daß er auch mit mir sei' (p.134); but her prayers are in vain. He leans to mysticism, supposing a god within whom there can be conflict (p.99), and may be a pantheist and vitalist: 'das alles ist lebig, so wie wir; es gibt nichts anderes; aber der liebe Gott ist überall! (p.121). In this as in the belief that God cannot upset His own laws Hauke agrees with Spinoza, a key forerunner of eighteenth-century rationalism: Storm fits him into a progressive history of ideas. Ironically, the obscurantist sectarians see his unorthodox thought as regressive, diabolical: 'Wer aber Gottes Allmacht widerstreitet...suchet den Feind Gottes, den Freund der Sünde, zu seinem Tröster' (p.101). The dyke-building is turned into devil's business, particularly when the *Schimmel* superstitions too come into play.

At the end religious themes recur. Storm prepares this not only by the various contributions to the argument about religion, but by repeated use of the actual word 'Gott'. Jewe Manners invokes God as the ally of the progressive: 'Bravo, Hauke Haien! Unser Herrgott wird dir dein Werk gelingen lassen!' (p.94). It is Elke's delirious 'O lieber Gott, ich seh ihn nimmer wieder!' (p.98) which impels Hauke to the notorious prayer; he notes Trin's deathbed utterance 'Gott gnad de annern!' (p.130) as perhaps prophetic; now in the storm he is confronted with the workman's 'Euere Schuld! Nehmt's mit vor Gottes Thron!' (p.140). Considering this he at last seems to become aware of what has been lacking in his strivings and addresses God — 'gleichsam der oberste Deichgraf, der von seinen Untergebenen Rechenschaft verlangt, über ihre Arbeit, nicht über ihre Moral' (*14*, p.64): 'Herr Gott,...ich habe meines Amtes schlecht gewartet!' (p.141). He promises to help his neighbours make good the damage, directly and for no personal gain. It is a practical, humane reaction, with overtones of religion: 'schlechte Jahre werden für die überschwemmten Fennen kommen...Wir müssen's tragen, und ich will helfen, auch denen, die mir Leid's getan...' (p.141). But the spirit of neighbourliness and forgiveness is overtaken by events. Having refused to make a concession to superstition by sacrificing a dog — when even Elke and Harke Jens would have given in to the folk-belief — he is now driven, with an echo of Trin's dying words, to make a greater sacrifice: 'Herr Gott, nimm mich; verschon die andern!' (p.143).

Religious self-sacrifice for the community has so far been even more alien to him than the altruism just mentioned. In now embracing it he loses his hubris and extinguishes the earthly self that had determined all his actions. We do not find out whether the final prayer is heard, but the going out of the lights seems to say not. 'Nacht', 'Tod', 'Nichts' have won. Storm is an unbeliever and cannot finally approve the Christian interpretation, though by repeated religious references he encourages the reader to think of Hauke's death as a metaphysically meaningful climax. It is tempting to resolve the paradox by positing that a religion other than Christianity is in Storm's mind; the obvious candidate is Germanic heathenism. Barz suggests that Hauke sacrifices himself to Wodan (*14*, p.67), and that with this Storm wishes to return the mythical dimension to a land only ever superficially converted to Christianity (*14*, p.76). But this is, I feel, to exaggerate. Storm was glad if his free inspiration turned out to be in harmony with the ways of thought of Germanic myth, but he was an atheist, not a closet pagan. When he wrote about a *Märchen* of his: 'Auch das spricht wohl für meine Dichtung, daß ich ganz instinktiv im Sinn und Geist der Germanischen Mythologie geschrieben' (to Hartmuth Brinkmann, 10 January 1866, *11*, II, p.149), the word *instinktiv* is the one to stress: he did not want to convert people to Wodanism!

8. Motifs

The story is full of motifs which have a double function: serving the description of circumstances or furthering the course of the plot, and suggesting a deeper layer of interpretation of the whole. The major motif, found already in Storm's source, and exploiting heathen elements of belief to connect Hauke with the devil, is the white horse, a sacred animal in Germanic myth; *Schimmelreiter* is defined by Meyer's encyclopaedia of 1890 as 'Im deutschen Volksmund so viel wie Wodan' (quoted *14*, p.76), the eternally wandering heathen god — thus, in a Christian view, demon or devil — with his *Wilde Jagd* (the phrase 'wilde Jagd' occurs in the text on the night of the catastrophe, p.136); Wodan legends were frequent into the the nineteenth century in North and East Germany. East Prussia, home of the story, has many such legends, superstitions and customs going back to a local equivalent to Wodan, Perkunas (*14*, p.181). The horse skeleton of unknown origin lying on Jeverssand — a connection with Trin' Jans's son and with the sea and death in general — is the first hint of the *Schimmel* (p.75); soon it is seen by moonlight restored to life. It disappears altogether (p.87) at the same time as Hauke brings a thin white horse home.

He bought the horse just after hearing that the dyke had been approved, when he was full of joy; twice it seemed to plead to be bought (pp.83f.), and he was rich enough. The horse seems to demand a share of his success and happiness, a necessary tax — to what authority? Similarly the stray dog will beg around the village before its fateful meeting with Hauke, (p.108). The vendor was a Slovak — that is, gipsy — with a hand like a claw and a laugh like a devil; the price Hauke pays (p.84) is another diabolical hint, a vague reminiscence of Judas's thirty pieces of silver. Elke hopes the devil has not rubbed off onto the horse. Hauke, in a common phrase with added meaning here, like

Elke's 'Hilf Himmel' (p.81), wants to prove he has made a 'Priesterhandel' (p.85). The horse seems one with him (p.85) and refuses to be ridden by Iven who comments 'den Schimmel reit' der Teufel!' (p.86), an echo of Carsten's words on seeing the horse on Jeverssand (pp.76f.). Iven's remark leaves Hauke — who has by now ridden the horse and already been allotted the role of unpredictable outsider and 'verteufelt' by the community (*20*, p.452) — little choice but to join himself to the devil in reply: 'Und ich!' (p.86). The horse tries to refuse when Hauke sacrifices himself (p.143); after its death the skeleton reappears on Jeverssand (p.144).

When Carsten comes to believe that the devil has taken over the skeleton and put it in Hauke's stable, he leaves to work for Ole Peters; stories which, somewhat justifiably, see Hauke as diabolical start circulating. Like Lucifer, the fallen angel become a devil, Hauke only brings human progress at the cost of risking the loss of any idea of a power higher than himself. Reason and hubris are inseparable; in having disavowed God, the rational man, Hauke, has become a devil. Thus one can see why religious-minded people attack Hauke after the so-called blasphemous prayer. But a converse interpretation is also possible: rather than the rational devil, the horse represents an irrational devil, and when it is one with Hauke, the dark, inexplicable side of existence has infiltrated his efforts. He is seen trying to behave as a leader should, praising those who work well — but they cannot hear the well-meant message, and the man who holds the horse is staring at it in dread (p.96), a significant scene. For Heybey (*23*, pp.14f.) the horse is a symbol of the instinctive, the id, all the negative sides of Hauke, which enable him to pursue his aims energetically, but demand their toll. 'Während der Menschengeist...im Werk der Dämmung seinen Endsieg vorzubereiten glaubt, verfällt Hauke...immer mehr unberechenbar-übervernünftigen Gewalten' (*39*, p.72). The more he tries to build up his life on reason, the deeper he falls into the grip of the daemonic and irrational. He is fighting 'die verkannte oder verleugnete Struktur des eigenen Daseins' (*39*, p.72). To sum up: whatever interpretation of the horse one favours, it is a key element of the story, having mythical overtones as well as deep bonds to Hauke's inward being.

The sea for Storm is always an elemental threat, never a beneficent provider; here it is an ever-present death-motif. It has also been thought, by Martini, to symbolise forces of fate, in man, nature and the supernatural, which break in and destroy despite all attempts at defence. The corpses of the drowned, and later on the animal bones on the islet, make it graphically clear that the sea is a force fickle and ungovernable, not to be trifled with, difficult to escape. Mirror-smooth and shining one day, mountainously threatening the next, it shows the duplicity or ambivalence of all natural phenomena (*16*, p.461). Wienke's fear of it seems a sign of her weakness: but she is right, seeing clearly the threat of the eternal irrational element.[5] In the delirium of the sick and dying the sea plays a great part. Elke in puerperal fever imagines herself threatened by floods. '"Wasser! Das Wasser!" wimmerte die Kranke. "Halt mich!..."' (p.98). It is a premonition, if imprecise, of the end of the story; the dying words of Trin' Jans refer both back to her son's death and forward to Hauke's: '...Hölp mi! Du bist ja bawen Water...Gott gnad de annern!' (p.130). In a way Hauke's constant battle to push back the sea is thus symbolic of a revolt against the dominion of death.

Elke, with her usual deeper sense, warns him when he suggests the new dyke: 'das ist ein Werk auf Tod und Leben' (p.71). But he is scarcely seeing clearly: 'Wie ein Rausch stieg es ihm ins Gehirn' (p.70) when he views the scene of his future triumphs. He has to force himself to look coolly and rationally at the work and its rewards. The overreaching exercise of reason in creating order out of chaos leads to an unreasoning intoxication, the negation of reason. Really consistent reasoning would lead to the conclusion that the sea cannot lightly be opposed. The individual cannot hope to cheat death; and there is always a greater or lesser element of hubris about the battle: man playing god, usurping the role of master of life and death.

Death is also a motif in its own right. In connection with the

[5] See William L. Cunningham, 'Zur Rolle des Wassers in Theodor Storms "Der Schimmelreiter"', *Germanic Notes* 13 (1982), 2-3.

funeral of Tede Volkerts, Storm quotes the epitaph of his father Volkert Tedsen to show that knowledge must decay, as must the individual and the family. Elke prays on this occasion (p.60): reason is silent before death. Here is an area of existence which Hauke, rational as he is, will have difficulty in mastering. He believes in a kind of immortality through the dyke which he intends to survive for 'hundert und aber hundert Jahre' (p.89). But his very success is based on old Volkers' death. And riding the horse, he is allied to forces of death and hell. Tragedy is at the basis of his life: progress rests on this treacherous ground. Not for long can Hauke stand proud and statuesque on his dyke, challenging man and nature; his own conflict and illness soon bring him to the point of slipping guiltily along it.

'The dyke provides a dramatic unity of place and action' (*33*, p.772). 'Meer und Deich, ungebändigte Naturgewalt und bändigende menschliche Leistung sind die zentralen Symbole der Novelle' (*19*, p.91). The dyke is a condition of life. If Hauke is punished at the end for neglect of his duty to it, this reflects an ancient punishment of being buried alive in the dyke as the penalty for neglect (*14*, p.49). The dyke is objectively useful and necessary, as some wiser villagers see: a work pleasing to God, done so as not to test His patience, a self-help against floods (pp.89f.); but understandably it is mainly seen as a means for Hauke's self-aggrandisement. It summarises the revolt against the sea and death, but becomes Luciferian when embarked on in the wrong spirit. Rogers (*32*, pp.189f.) views it as a symbol intended by Hauke, the bodily sign of his rightness, success, even immortality. If it succeeds, he cannot fail. He seems to attribute impossible powers of both physical and metaphysical protection to it; its association with his name long after his death vindicates him. He cannot bring himself to condone its breaching in the flood, though he previously saw this as the rational act in such an emergency.

The ash tree before the house, a reminder of the Nordic tree of life, Yggdrasil, perhaps, planted by Elke's father, succeeding the one planted by her great-grandfather, 'der erste Deichgraf des Geschlechtes' (p.25), accompanies events closely — notably the scene in which Hauke and Elke discuss their fathers' advancing

age, and Hauke cannot help welcoming Tede Volkerts'
approaching death, which will open the way to Elke (pp.50f.).
The tree seems about to split (p.134) in the final storm, thus
sharing the family's fate.

9. Trin' Jans and Others

A set of motifs with conflicting interpretations is provided by Trin' Jans, a figure richly illustrative of social circumstances, who can be seen as a mother figure or a witch. She is marked out as an exception in living outside the village. As mother of a dead son she perhaps represents a suffering maternal, emotional and female element, threatened by the rational, violent masculinity of a Hauke. She sets her cat — her last surviving relative as it were, inherited from her son — above Tede's whole farm, insisting on the emotional and physical warmth it gives her; she still has its skin at the end (p.112). She is seen mothering unfortunate creatures: Claus, Wienke, Perle. It has even been claimed that her story of the mermaid is more than superstition, symbolising 'das Elend des vereinsamten Menschen in einer vom Egoismus des Mannes beherrschten Welt' (*19*, p.89). In this interpretation, her last words, prefiguring Hauke's, show that she has long reached the state of unselfishness he only comes to in his last moments. But this, like much else in *Schimmelreiter* criticism, remains a speculation with little basis in the text.

Trin' and her cat do not really fit into the schoolmaster's story, with its concentration on the rational hero. But the less rational events of the second half have to be prepared at least a little. And in terms of Hauke's life the killing of the cat is significant because it takes place after Hauke's confirmation and marks in concrete terms, as the confirmation does abstractly, his emergence into adulthood. If previously he idled on the dykes and killed birds aimlessly, now he kills a bird that he wants to keep, clinging to it as later he clings to the idea of the new dyke. And the argument with Trin' leads to his leaving home because there is not room there for two men: he has grown up.

The asocial Hauke is close enough to the cat to think of
training it as a retriever; he gives it plovers he has killed with
stones, a very masculine pastime; but it is a male too, whose
natural greed he disregards, and when he refuses it a kingfisher
there is bound to be a fight. Thus a suppressed layer of violence in
him, 'Ein Grimm, wie gleichfalls eines Raubtiers' (p.19), comes
to light. A number of Storm's protagonists are similarly
described as wild beasts rather than men: notably Hans Kirch (in
Hans und Heinz Kirch), the ambitious materialist, and Sternow
(in *Der Herr Etatsrat*), the cruel alcoholic. 'Hauke ist eine
Mischung aus Etatsrat und Hans Kirch' (*17*, p.90): obsessive,
inebriated with his own rightness.

Trin' takes the cat's body to Tede Haien. A slight ambiguity
of presentation serves Storm's aims here: 'sie streichelte das
dicke Fell des toten Tieres, legte ihm die Tatzen zusammen,
neigte ihre lange Nase über dessen Kopf und raunte ihm
unverständliche Zärtlichkeiten in die Ohren' (p.21). The actions
express feelings of which we have already been told abstractly
(p.19). Mention of her long nose is slightly ridiculous and adds a
little irony to the touching scene; but it also hints distantly that
she is a witch. The words she 'raunte' suggest this too — some
sort of spell? But no, they are tender words. Storm holds the
balance between suggesting that there is something eerie about
Trin', showing her as a pitiable lonely old woman, and holding
her up to ridicule (as Hauke no doubt would, had he any spark
of levity): a balance important to the story as a whole.

Hauke offers Trin' a gentler cat (p.20); Tede gives her money
to buy a lambskin — satisfying her body, not her soul — and
offers her the best of his cat's next litter. These promises are
apparently never kept. The cat dead, rats get into Trin's back
yard (p.32) and she starts a poultry yard on the dyke road at the
front; she says there are too many rats 'in euren Gräben' (p.44)
— perhaps connected with the ruin of the old dyke by mice later
(p.123). Hauke has altered the balance of nature by killing the
cat; the new dyke will also upset an ecological balance. He plans
changes with no sense of their wider consequences (*18*, p.165).

After his good throw in *Eisboseln* (p.43) Trin' offers
reconciliation to Hauke, but he seems not to grasp the meaning

of her gesture, and gives her money. The old Trin' has a feeling of revenge because she cursed Hauke and now he has an idiot child; the reconciliation appears to have been revoked. She pities Wienke too, and tries to bring some warmth into her life, but also seems a threat to the Haien family as she diverts her affection to herself. Trin' in old age may have been suggested by an old woman, Lena Koch, mentioned by Storm: '...dabei sammelte ich Sagen und Volksglauben und Märchen...;...zu einer alten halbverrückten Person, die in einem unsrer Hinterhäuser in einem zimmerartigen Verschlage haust, bin ich Abends mehrmals gegangen, um mir unter den sonderbarsten Exclamationen und Gebehrden Stücke von ihr erzählen zu lassen. Dabei schnurrte...das Spinnrad, der Kater lag unter dem Ofen und schnarchte wie ein Kind;...auf dem Tisch brannte eine Thranlampe — vollkommener Hexenapparat.' (1 December 1842, *8*, p.40).

Trin's crooked hand and stick, spinning-wheel, cat and mysterious knowledge of water sprites and cursed monsters, with the catastrophes following her death, form the evidence for her being a witch. If the cat is her familiar, Claus must be seen as 'symbolically fulfilling the role of Trin's messenger or go-between with the other world' (*13*, pp.6f.). When she curses Hauke (p.19), there is little sign yet that the curse should be taken too seriously. But Hauke walks 'auf dem Deich der Stadt zu' (p.20) — something repeated later (p.68) where he takes up an earlier idea of building a new dyke. Is the new dyke a result of Trin's curse? On the whole, the evidence is not enough for us to view Trin' as a witch — how does she manage without a living cat as familiar all those years? — but Storm undoubtedly meant his hints to heighten the atmosphere. Claus is possibly ridden down by Hauke at the end (p.136). At the *Eisboseln*, the course of his throw was hidden by a gull: 'Hauke has his eye on a distant goal, which is obscured momentarily by a part of the natural scene' (*18*, p.165). Now, Ellis says, he tramples the gull because he is looking ahead, to the dyke. The circle of Trin's animals is completed by Perle, the dog which like the horse is of unknown origin (p.108), becomes Wienke's companion, and goes with her and Elke to their death (p.142).

To Artiss, the birds mentioned in the text are significant: 'at one with the mysterious force which controls the world' (*13*, p.14). Crows and gulls met on the shore by the frame narrator already show that everything in the story comes from the sea and is maleficent; the gulls seem connected with the souls of the guilty dead; their complaining cries close to people and houses are a common ill omen (*13*, pp.5f.). Between killing Trin's cat and killing her gull, Hauke can show humanity; but the accident with Claus exacts revenge according to a belief widespread in coastal areas: 'the irrational, chaotic other world has claimed its own' (*13*, p.7).

The ghostly figures which Hauke sees on the mudflats, refuses to fear and tells no one about (p.15f.) are much later interpreted by Hauke as birds (p.121); refusal to believe in evil spirits is part of his pantheism. Artiss again finds these birds, herons and crows, significant, citing their use as ill omens — but also quoting the Jungian view of their link with the Earth Mother (*13*, pp.8f.). The kingfisher and osprey are also examined for symbolic meanings; the peewit, also a bird of ill omen, which rises from the horse's skull, is 'a demonic messenger from the other world, sent to reveal the genesis of the white horse' (*13*, p.11). Happier birds such as larks are rarely met. The choice of black and white birds underlines the duality Storm insists on: both white gulls and black crows are in Artiss's reading omens of death (*13*, p.16), but wild birds are also 'symbols of release and liberation' (*13*, p.16). Artiss's interpretation gives much food for thought, but is too self-contradictory for one to feel that it has in the last analysis deepened one's understanding of Storm.

10. Der Schimmelreiter *as* Novelle

'...der bereits vom Tode gezeichnete, aber jugendlich
aufbrechende Storm schafft mit dem "Schimmelreiter" seine
größte Novelle und mit ihr vielleicht sogar die bedeutendste
Realisierung dieser Gattung überhaupt' (*19*, p.11). The term
Novelle — the imperfectly naturalised English equivalent would
be 'novella' or 'novelle' — designates a type of short story much
cultivated in German literature of the nineteenth century and by
Storm in particular. This is not the place to discuss the varying
critical definitions of the *Novelle* (the reader may consult
Swales, *35*, and Ellis, *18*). But a short, apodictic survey of the
generic characteristics of the *Novelle* that seem to me important
for an understanding of our text may be useful. The *Novelle* is
longer than a mere anecdote, but shorter than all but the shortest
novels: Storm recommended 'vierzig, höchstens fünfzig Seiten
von Ihrer gewöhnlichen Briefschrift' (to Hermione von
Preuschen and Mina Hahn, 26 October 1873, *11*, II, p.73). The
adaptation in Germany of the Italian term *novella* fulfilled the
need 'for a way of grouping together those literary productions
which were most characteristic of that age in that community'
(*18*, p.19); in a land of small towns and a scattered
Bildungsbürgertum the literary periodical, with its freight of
short stories, was a major means of cultural dissemination.

Its subjects may be ambitious ones, extreme individual experiences: love, the inspiration and function of the artist, the
supernatural or inexplicable — though some purists would
banish such subjects into the genre of *Märchen* —, natural
disasters, mass movements, insanity, threats to existence or to
honour or self-esteem. The term *Novelle* rather than a more
general one such as *Kurzgeschichte* is intended to denote a
certain aesthetic rigour and distinguish real works of art from
inferior kinds of prose narrative which threatened to debase the

coinage. Storm did not work to any set theory of how the ideal
Novelle should look, but on the basis of a canon — constantly
changing, as he and others produced innovative examples — of
works generally accepted in their own time as *Novellen*. Yet he
and his contemporaries did see the genre as having its own
tradition, characteristic features and norms. The common
ground of their definitions was that it 'is concerned with a
single, striking event and is thus a realistic genre which displays
artistic concentration together with objective narrative' (*18*,
p.11). Action is more important than characterisation; too full a
treatment of the social background is eschewed; digressions and
extraneous material must be removed to concentrate on a single
subject: 'in einem *einzigen* Kreise einen *einzelnen* Conflict, eine
sittliche oder Schicksals-Idee oder ein entschieden abgegrenztes
Charakterbild'.[6]

In Storm's day two features especially were seen as touch-
stones of the *Novelle*. Tieck insisted on a single, surprising
turning-point (*Wendepunkt*) of the plot; Heyse required, or was
generally taken to require, that the *Novelle* should have at its
centre a *Dingsymbol*, which is both concretely necessary to the
plot and also symbolic, and so gives physical shape to the
abstract theme of the story. Indeed *Novellen* generally contain
some elements of symbol or motif, which may also take a role in
the plot or in the depiction of places and characters; it is inherent
in the genre, with its intensity, that certain things necessary to
the plot also attract associations which make us see them as
symbolic. But Tieck's and Heyse's theories are of little heuristic
value (*18*, pp.5ff.). Despite the requirement of a single turning-
point, a few fictional 'biographies' qualify as *Novellen*: Stifter's
Brigitta, Droste-Hülshoff's *Die Judenbuche*, and *Der
Schimmelreiter* have fairly full characterisation and background
and the complete story of a life, but also concentrate on a single
theme or episode — here the dyke-building and its consequences
— and use a fulness of motifs. Detailed characterisation does
become increasingly acceptable in the *Novelle*, up to Thomas

[6] Paul Heyse, introduction to his collection *Deutscher Novellenschatz*, Vol.1
(Munich, 1871), quoted in *2*, pp.87f.

Mann's *Der Tod in Venedig*. But it is sometimes doubted whether the long tales of the late nineteenth century are still *Novellen*, even if they show generic features; some contemporary novels are scarcely longer than *Der Schimmelreiter* and use a single episode as centre, as for example Raabe's *Stopfkuchen*. Thus a *Novelle* is not defined by whether we today discern in it certain formal characteristics, but by whether it struck the contemporaries as standing in the line of development of the *Novelle*.

It is vital to the *Novelle* that human experience be interpreted, that the striking event be placed 'in the context of a generality of human affairs and their understanding' (*35*, p.56). Perhaps the genre's charm for the writer is in the challenge of the isolated event to the interpretative faculties: the author tries to make sense of chance and circumstance, to show that they are really providence or destiny, to prove that an individual with a critical and unafraid attitude to the world can make his experience of catastrophe a meaningful, perhaps tragic, one; or to explore 'odd moments when the restraints of social order are challenged by new experiential dimensions' (*35*, p.34). Such essays of interpretation are offered by the writer to his reader, perhaps with some irony, as shedding light on phenomena which may be at the edges of our social and metaphysical experience.

The complications about the narrator and the frame which are typical of Storm and prominent in *Der Schimmelreiter* fit in here. The author decides how much the narrator knows, finds important, understands, and tells the reader; he uses the narrator to introduce a certain distance from the events, and perhaps to hint ironically at connections which would be unduly banal or frankly incredible if stated baldly. By convention the narrator has the 'ability to read other people's minds, to be present during conversations which could not have been overheard, to show extraordinary powers of memory, and so on' (*18*, p.28). The frame introduces the reader to a different set of circumstances, those of the narrator's own life and times, and raises the question of how the plot events were regarded in those circumstances, thus giving us a different perspective on the inner plot and deepening our interpretation of it. 'The *Rahmen* is a structural principle that involves the interplay of what is narrated and the effect that this narrative act has on the world to which it is directed' (*35*, p.54).

The *Novelle* aims in Storm's interpretation at the tight logic, the fixed structure, the stylistic purity of a five-act tragedy.

> Sie ist nicht mehr, wie einst, 'die kurzgehaltene Darstellung einer durch ihre Ungewöhnlichkeit fesselnden und einen überraschenden Wendepunkt darbietenden Begebenheit'; die heutige Novelle ist die Schwester des Dramas und die strengste Form der Prosadichtung. Gleich dem Drama behandelt sie die tiefsten Probleme des Menschenlebens; gleich diesem verlangt sie zu ihrer Vollendung einen im Mittelpunkte stehenden Konflikt, von welchem aus das Ganze sich organisiert, und demzufolge die geschlossenste Form und die Ausscheidung alles Unwesentlichen; sie duldet nicht nur, sie stellt auch die höchsten Forderungen der Kunst.[7]

Storm shares his era's views on action versus characterisation, the need for conflict, and the concentration on a single centre. But Tieck's and Heyse's specific criteria for the *Novelle* help little with *Der Schimmelreiter*: the demand for a *Wendepunkt* remains unanswered, for there is either no surprise, or a series of surprises, or a surprise placed right at the end where it cannot be said to *turn* the plot; the requirement of a *Dingsymbol*, which Storm respected (to Heyse, 16 April 1876, *6*, II, p.11), may or may not be realised in the dyke, or the white horse, or both. Perhaps for such reasons Storm did not care to claim a place in the *Novelle* tradition for the story and modestly suggested *Eine Deichgeschichte* or *Eine Geschichte aus dem Marsch* (to Ferdinand Tönnies, 7 April 1888, *11*, II, p.386). But if we set the specific criteria aside and consider the wider development of the genre, we need have no such scruples.

Much of Storm's earlier work, such as *Immensee*, and that of

---

[7] *Eine zurückgezogene Vorrede aus dem Jahre 1881*, intended for Vol.11 of Storm's *Gesammelte Werke*, quoted in *2*, p.90.

other writers (for example Keller's *Kleider machen Leute*) falls
into a pattern of the hero failing to assert himself; the
Wendepunkt if discernible comes when he can no longer sustain
his individuality against hostile circumstances and has to submit
and become an ordinary member of society. Freund has argued
that this structure is typical of the *Novelle*, but that *Der
Schimmelreiter* for most of its length is rather an example of another
characteristic genre of the prose literature of the era, the
Entwicklungsroman. In an era which believes in man as maker
and master of his own fate, and in great individuals as moulders
of a collective fate, a biographical literary form — the story of
the formative influences on a remakable character — is naturally
popular. Here Hauke, a man of practical action, ruler of his
own decisions, develops his individuality and rises to the
execution of an excelling work. But as soon as he discovers the
reappearance of the *Priel* all is reversed. He is no longer in
charge. The tragedy which sets in at this point makes the work
veer away from the *Entwicklungsroman* towards the *Novelle*
and opens our eyes retrospectively to all the flaws of character in
Hauke which Freund thinks a true *Entwicklungsroman* would
have ironed out by now: egoism, calculation, violence,
arrogance, thoughtlessnes. 'Was romanhaft einsetzte, endet
novellistisch, der Aufstieg des Helden mündet in sein Scheitern'
(*19*, p.102).

Though this interpretation uses too optimistic a concept of
Entwicklungsroman, the view that *Der Schimmelreiter* is more
than half novel should be taken seriously. For Himmel the break
comes with the decision to build the dyke: at that point the
actual *Novelle*, based on the sequence 'Forderung nach einem
Opfer — Verhinderung des Hundeopfers — Selbstopfer
Haukes',[8] begins. We may note that this coincides with the
teacher's remarks about the change in sources for the rest of the
story (pp.74f.; see following chapter). References forward from
early motifs assure some continuity across the structural divide:
the *Seeteufel* taken up when Hauke gives Wienke the rational

---

[8] Hellmuth Himmel, *Geschichte der deutschen Novelle* (Berne and Munich: Francke, 1963), p.293.

explanation for them, the return of the Trin' Jans motifs. Inner cohesion is given in that the early characterisation of Hauke, as one who always holds on to what he has — defending his bird against the cat at the cost of injury —, is still valid at the end: he assures the survival of *his* new fen at the cost of his life.

It has also been claimed that the second half of the story can be separated into two strands, one of which invites us to see Hauke as a positive hero in a continuation of the schoolmaster's *Entwicklungsroman*, whilst the other is made up of borrowings from an implicit narrator, Antje Vollmers (see following chapter). This argument too leads to the conclusion that the work is on the borders of *Novelle* and novel: Storm came from the *Novelle* tradition, but his complex view of the world as it had developed by the late 1880s could not be expressed without exceeding the limits which nineteenth-century practice set to the genre. But it has been argued that precisely the second strand, with its unrealistic elements, takes the work away from the *Novelle* genre, presumably towards ghost story. Storm would not have agreed, having encouraged Heyse to include tales 'die ins Phantastische hinaufsteigen' in the *Deutscher Novellenschatz* (to Heyse, 30 October 1872, *6*, I, p.49), though feeling they are hybrids. He draws the line only at pure allegory.

The controversies about the status of *Der Schimmelreiter* as a *Novelle* help us to focus on some interesting points of structure and intention, but when the dust has cleared it seems more natural to consider the story as a *Novelle* and as a major achievement in one of the mainstreams of German realism, than to place it in some category — *Märchen*, *Kurzgeschichte* or *Entwicklungsroman* — where it can have only peripheral status.

11. The Narrative Structure

Der Schimmelreiter is famous for its complex narrative structure. 'Profundity and cogency of tragic thought are matched...by high excellence of form' (*33*, p.770); the structure brings about a balance of subjective and objective, lyric and epic, involvement and distance (*30*, p.662). In an outer frame (p.3) the authorial narrator proposes to recount something he read in an old magazine. This frame is left open, not referred back to again. It serves to arouse the reader's interest. Storm does not claim a special importance or renewed topicality for the old story, but assumes that a tale that has remained in the memory for fifty years must have some interest. His situation long ago in his great-grandmother's room hints to the reader that he too may take up such a comfortable, receptive attitude; an appeal to the attraction of the good old days is implied. Caught up in the fast-moving life of his own day, the reader will relax in a story of the pre-industrial age and at the same time renew his connection with his historical roots. The implication that the author is now a wise old man also suggests that in retelling the old story he may offer some interpretative insight into life in general.

The inner frame, to be thought of as set not long before the magazine article, thus in the 1830s, forms the next stage in the gradual return to the time of the happenings proper: Storm gives the idea that the story happened in the distant past, yet not so distant that there cannot be bridges of personal experience and oral transmission between it and his own time (his great-grandmother would have been a girl in 1756). This frame also determines the mood: an important function, as our interpretation of its events will colour our view of the story as a whole. Here in a realm reminiscent of *Märchen*, deserted, uncertainly lit by a moon troubled by scudding clouds, bordered by a heaving sea, the secondary narrator — the writer of the item in the old magazine — sees the ghost white horse rider. The story behind this, told by the teacher, is a legend, whose value lies more in its function for the people who continually retell and rehear it than in any biographical truth about Hauke it contains. The incompatibility of elements may be structurally important: 'What Hauke was really like is not the point; the narrative scheme stresses...that this is not a story of Hauke, but a local legend in which fact and fiction cannot be disentangled. The point of legends is the ideas they embody, not the distant and shadowy figures that are their historical source; and so the story is as much concerned with the attitudes of its co-narrators, their part in the creation of the legend, as it is with Hauke' (*18*, p.37).

By shifting the time back from the 1880s to the age of the teacher narrator, and thence to the previous century, Storm prepares the reader to suspend disbelief in the paranormal elements. The frame shows that there is no definitive historical truth: we can only interpret data which remain veiled and incomplete. Storm presents us with the story on these terms: 'So geschah es im achtzehnten Jahrhundert; so wurde es geglaubt im neunzehnten; seht zu, was ihr selbst damit anfängt!' (*16*, p.465). The reader has to face and answer the question of the existence of a ghost without unambiguous guidance from the text. The community of the 1830s clearly believes in the paranormal phenomena and lets them influence its actions. Against the weight of the schoolmaster's logic it is sometimes hard to believe in them; but he cannot claim complete authority. The story is not his but has been passed down orally for seventy years or so; he has bonded together material from different sources and put his stamp on it. The traveller narrator, now taking the role of a critical listener, promises to keep an open attitude to it and sort out the wheat from the chaff himself; accordingly he makes no comment, engages in no discussion at the end; when the frame *Deichgraf* claims that the breach in the dyke on the other shore vindicates the ghost story, he shrugs his shoulders and proposes to sleep on the problem (p.145). The next morning he resumes his interrupted journey. The reader, Storm means to suggest, may well also feel, although the lapse of time since 1756 seems to promise a chance of seeing the hero dispassionately, that there is no easy answer.

A number of interruptions of the story belong to the inner frame. The first (p.9) is the schoolmaster's comment on the anecdote about a Dutch Euclid told both of Hans Momsen and of Hauke; this implies — a common ploy of historical fiction — that Hauke is of the same degree of reality as Momsen. Then there are the teacher's remarks meant to reduce the tension of the eerie situation at the point just reached — the supposed sea-ghosts. During this pause the *Schimmelreiter* is seen outside, a further eerie element which the teacher treats coolly. He succeeds in making the traveller unsure whether he in fact saw anything. At the next interruption, a late addition by Storm in the manuscript, when on the report of the rider's plunge into the pool the others leave and the view out of the window is clear, only hurrying clouds are visible: the fantastic is pushed into the background, giving a counterweight to the following more supernatural part of the story (p.55). The move to the schoolmaster's scholarly retreat (p.56) too reinforces the rational; and it discourages further external interruptions and heightens the intensity and concentration of the story.

Almost exactly half-way through comes the teacher's remark that the sources of his narration, from this point on, are common winter evening talk (pp.74f.). He contrasts his own researches into the story, which claim reliability, and the loose talk of the village. The implicit theme is the conflict, not resolved by the narration, of fact and superstition. A final short parenthesis (p.129) mentions the date of the events, thus insisting on the historical reality, but also on the distance in time from us, of the story. The inner frame ends (p.144f.) with an appendix on the fate of the bodies, the importance of Hauke and the lessons of the story. The teacher sheds gentle doubt on the claim that everyone in the village saw the skeleton on Jeverssand again afterwards, contrasted with the indisputable deaths of Hauke and his wife and child. Drawing the curtain back, he reveals the landscape again: we are returned to the 'present'.

Within the inner frame (p.8) there is a hint that a different narrator from the schoolmaster, namely a character who never appears, the old housekeeper Antje Vollmers, would tell the story differently. Her version would be seen less from the teacher's Hauke-centred perspective, more from that of another old woman, Trin' Jans; and more in line with the popular view of the story of Hauke, in which he figures as 'Spuk und Nacht-gespenst' (p.145). This again encourages the reader to make up his or her own mind about the plausibility of the supernatural elements. Storm's problem of making a ghost story respectable is in effect made part of the story. He treads a narrow path between giving way to the, rationalistically speaking, impossible, and taking all the mystery out of events. In the talk in the inn the proponent of rational interpretations is the schoolmaster, the *Deichgraf* champions belief in the ghost. The superstitious people let the schoolmaster tell the story, implying respect for his position; the younger ones seem keener on the idea, being perhaps less superstitious than their elders, a sign of progress; but he in turn is unable to expunge the inexplicable from his narration, though wishing to hem in superstition wherever possible. If one sees the events of the story rationalistically, one believes that author and internal narrator are rationalists too; if one prefers the irrational, one posits that the implied narrator Antje Vollmers would have given a deeper, more complex view than the over-intellectual schoolmaster. The truth is somewhere in the middle: Storm sees both the incompleteness of the teacher's world view, and the dis-advantages of letting superstition and obscurantism have their own way.

He does not let Antje narrate. Instead he describes the teacher in ways that predispose us to believe him as intelligent, kind, serious, the best storyteller present, and so entrusts the story to a man with a vested interest in enlightenment, whose didactic aim in the story is to explore conflicting elements of Hauke: his rationality in theory and practice, his insensitivity in personal relations. He tells the story authoritatively, choosing which times, places and episodes to present fully; claiming omniscience, despite his claim that the story has documentary value; filling out the record with the thoughts and private conversations of Hauke and his father and Elke. In his self-interruptions he comments on the story and the way of telling it; this turns his narration into a demonstration, a story presented in a form which enables the hearer to turn its lessons to advantage. He like Hauke is described as 'hager' (p.8), though small where Hauke is tall; both are 'men of book-learning' (*18*, p.159) devoted to improvement and reason. He identifies to some extent with Hauke, as a progressive intellectual. But he has failed to achieve his early ambitions 'einer verfehlten Brautschaft wegen' (p.8), whereas Hauke achieved his by marrying Elke, so he may envy Hauke his success and achievements (*18*, pp.159ff.). His position, sympathising but spared the great fall which attends a great rise, is somewhat like that of the chorus in a classical tragedy (*23*, p.8). Like Zeitblom in Thomas Mann's *Doktor Faustus*, he filters the daemonic through an undaemonic medium.[9]

Thus he approves of Hauke's refusal to be afraid of the sea-ghosts, which precedes his recognition that they are merely birds. Indeed, in this episode he purposely sets up an apparent instance of the supernatural, only in order to knock it down triumphantly and impose the lesson that the individual may not be able to reason enough to free himself from superstition at once, but will progress if he has a correct attitude. Originally too Storm had him tell another twist to the ending (printed and commented on in *25*), a parody of the *Gruselgeschichte* genre. Here the irrational is carried to the point of absurdity: Carsten tells Vollina he was on the dyke and saw the dying Hauke being carried off by the devil. And the teacher tentatively interprets the ghost as a being very much alive, an eccentric local meteorologist who is fond of riding up and down the dykes in storms. This would do away with the whole paranormal content, if one thought the local people too stupid to recognise a local man, and if one dismissed the repeated accounts of the rider plunging into the site of the breach. While the people, Carsten and Vollina, are seen as even more credulous than before, the teacher produces new evidence for his rationalist interpretation to

---

[9] R.M. Browning, 'Association and Disassociation in Storm's Novellen', *Publications of the Modern Language Association* 66 (1951), 381-404, here 403.

balance things out. But Storm, finding this passage at variance with the mood of the final pages, cut it. He salvaged only the cool statement that the skeleton was again seen on Jeverssand afterwards.

Does the uncanny horse grazing on the islet remain a horse all the time that Carsten spends investigating it, as Iven sees, or is it a skeleton, as Carsten says (pp.79f.)? Storm insists equally on the repeated observations and the unwillingness to believe in the apparition at first — 'Vielleicht auch ist es nur ein Schaf...' (p.77) — and in the dubiety of the whole — 'was sie für ein Pferd, einen Schimmel, hielten...' (p.77); '...wie weiße Wasserstreifen schien es mitunter über die Erscheinung hinzuziehen' (p.80). The reader must judge what credence to attach to the reports of uneducated men, based on experiences of misty nights — but there are two occasions and two observers, whose attitudes later crystallise out as very different: Iven unconcerned, Carsten obsessed with the reality of the horse (p.87). Thus the schoolmaster is forced to witness against himself: he cannot, as he would like to, tell a rational, documentary version of the story, since the story would not exist but for the well-attested uncanny elements.

As with Iven and Carsten, so with the traveller narrator, whom we are predisposed to take as an authority, like the teacher narrator. He sees the ghost spontaneously and at first hand, though he cagily uses the word 'Erscheinung' for it; details like the sharp eyes and flying coat may add to the atmosphere but do not clinch the matter. The silence and obscurity of the meeting with the rider — was there anything at all? Has he plunged into the pool? — make for an imprecise, speculative narration. But what he thinks he sees accords with general experience; it is not just a fantasy. The ghost exists: a friendly and useful one whose function is to serve the cause of beating back the sea, just as surely as the dyke does. The test of an experience is in its fruits. Hauke Haien is both the rationalist creator of a dyke still standing, and the irrational warner frequently seen. The white horse was not, or not only, a creature of the devil.

Storm accepts the paranormal elements; a purely rational

interpretation leaves gaps. Trin's curse, the horse's skeleton, the gipsy, the general belief that Hauke is in league with the devil, cannot be dismissed lightly. The schoolmaster as a rationalist does not have the last word. There is an uncanny order of reality which irrupts into everyday reality. Certainly any attempt at a one-dimensional view of the events of the story is bound to result in a dangerously lop-sided picture of Storm's intentions. Freund, for example, argues that Storm intends us to disbelieve the apparent occult phenomena in the story, to emancipate ourselves from the irrational; and this implies, according to Freund, that Storm wishes us to take advantage of the chances offered by post-1871 Germany — we should replace twilight *Innerlichkeit* by the light of a new start, the sunshine as the traveller rides to the town symbolising this. But this argument seems very wide of the mark in its wilful disregard of the care Storm took to balance the rational and irrational elements.

The schoolmaster's story has been seen as a five-act tragedy (*39*, p.85; *23*, pp.9ff.): I. Hauke's childhood and loneliness; II. a sort of apprenticeship in old Volkerts' house; III. the climax of Hauke's hubris as an excrescence of his egocentricity; IV. the completion of the great work; V. the supernal forces' reply and destruction of the hero. I see it rather as bipartite: the break is between Hauke's development up to the decision to build the new dyke, and the building of the dyke and what follows, and is marked by the self-interruption (p.74) just about half-way through the story. We have in the first half heard only of events and conversations involving Tede, Hauke and Elke (*21*, p.556). From the mid-point on, the emphasis is different. More elements not directly experienced by Hauke have to be included in order to explain his problems: the episode of the horse on Jeverssand is something he never knows about. In a short space we now have that story, the approval of the dyke plans and the buying of the horse; some would say that henceforth, despite the apparent success of the dyke-building, Hauke personally is doomed. Another set of ominous events within a short space runs from the start of the dyke works (p.95), through Wienke's birth, Elke's illness and premonition of the end, and Hauke's 'blasphemous prayer', to the completion of the dyke. The eerie and supernatural themes of the white horse, blasphemy, omens, natural signs take over; rational complexes like those of the first half are lacking. Superstitious ideas are presented as probable, if not actually corroborated. The idea of Hauke as ghost is prepared intensively up to the catastrophic end (*27*, pp.122-24). Alien elements break through. All contributes to the feeling of doom.

Storm carefully places in his narrative high and low points of Hauke's development. Victory in *Eisboseln*, quickly followed by the dance and the buying of a ring, is an example of a high point, as is the endorsement of his ambition by his dying father. Low points are killing the cat, deceiving himself about the state of the dyke, and so on. And material that leads one to sympathise with Hauke alternates with episodes that show him in a bad light. The high point of the second half is easily discerned just about half-way through it, when Hauke hears workers calling the new fen 'Hauke-Haien-Koog' (p.110). His reaction to this oversteps the line between honest pride and hubris; and immediately the ominous Trin' begins to take a more prominent role, incidentally lending colour to the thought that the schoolmaster is by now unwillingly borrowing from Antje Vollmers' version.

The downward pull of reactionary forces, personal weakness and stress leads to a catastrophe affecting Hauke, his family and the community. But Hauke's death in the flood is not a foregone conclusion. In his final ride, when he formulates the morally good intention of redressing his isolation from the villagers by helping repair their losses, the social and ethical elements are brought back to the forefront. But then the unexplained death of Elke and Wienke is the culmination of a series of prophecies, forebodings and references to a sacrifice which Storm has carefully accumulated. The schoolmaster's and Antje's stories overlap without necessarily contradicting one another: the former aims to recount the building of the dyke, the latter the genesis of the ghost; with the buying of the horse immediately after official approval for building the dyke is received, the two strands are intimately interwoven. The paranormal turns out to have real and fatal significance, but the apocalyptic machinery would not have been set in motion had not Elke and Wienke inexplicably left the safety of their home.

12. Language, Style and Symbolism

The story proceeds in quasi-dramatic scenes with groups, individuals, sound-effects, tableaux, emotional tension. Sounds of nature and sounds of men's work are more prominent than dialogue, culminating in the thundering of the sea at Hauke's death. A short but telling example of the scene is when a woman tells Tede Haien about the corpses recovered from the sea:

> ...draußen am offenen Haf auf den gefrorenen Watten hatten sie gelegen. Ein junges Weib, die dabeigewesen war, als man sie in das Dorf geholt hatte, stand redselig vor dem alten Haien: "Glaubt nicht, daß sie wie Menschen aussahen", rief sie; "nein, wie die Seeteufel! So große Köpfe", und sie hielt die ausgespreizten Hände von weitem gegeneinander...' (p.14).

We do not see the woman arrive: she is as it were there when the curtain rises, is characterised in one word and delivers a speech attended by gesture. Despite the plasticity of such episodes, the tone throughout is remarkably even. The schoolteacher, taking no account of the different phases of the plot, carefully records the passage of seasons and years — though he seems to slip when Hauke deals with the Martinmas accounts on a 'Maiabend' (p.30) — recounting happenings almost entirely in chronological order, episode by episode, without apparent ornament.

Storm writes with careful realism. The many technical and local terms of dyking, the shore and farming anchor the events in reality and give local colour. So do Low German words — *Plattdeutsch* had come in in the seventeenth century as a language to use with the Dutch immigrants who could not master the dialects of Friesian (*14*, p.116) — or their transcription into standard German, such as 'Uns' Weert' (p.32) as a mode of address to one's employer, 'Brüche' (p.33), a fine, 'hohl Ebbe' (p.127), the lowest state of the tide, occurring with a north-east wind, or 'Brummeis' (p.42), thin ice from beneath which the water has run off. Especially telling, and typical of Storm, is the old cautionary verse on the grave of Volkert Tedsen (p.59). Local peculiarities such as the 'Beilegerofen' . (p.61), a stove let into the wall at the back, or the clay pipes brought out for the funeral guests (p.62), add to the atmosphere. The description of the *Deichgraf*'s living-room with its 'dauerhafte Tapete' of tiles (p.26) is a piece of *Kulturgeschichte*; so are the linen shirts and woollen stockings that form part of Hauke's pay (p.29), or Elke's 'Vogelstricken' (p.31). Slow social change is exemplified by a dance, the 'Zweitritt, der eben erst hier in die Mode gekommen war' (p.47). The *Boselspiel* prominent in the story holds a place in local culture. Of Elke's *Tracht*, the economical author mentions only the 'Spitzenstrich des goldbrokatenen Käppchens' (p.59). But the amount of description in the first half supports the theory that the story starts out as a novel. The schoolmaster often motivates explanations by presuming that local terms are new to the traveller: thus Trin' Jans, visiting Tede, descends 'den Akt, wie man bei uns die Trift- und Fußwege nennt...' (p.20).

Slight archaisms remind us that the story is set in the previous century. Modes of address, for instance, are chosen according to the customs of the times (*40*, pp.9f.). The third person substituted for the second to emphasise a social gap between speaker and hearer, as in Tede Haien's invitation to Trin', 'halt Sie das Maul' (p.22), is evocatively archaic. Storm anticipates the transition in the later eighteenth and early nineteenth centures (*24*, p.60) from use of patronymic names (Volkert Tedsen's son has the surname Volkerts) to inheritable surnames (Tede Haien's son is called Haien, not Tedsen). We find 'ihren künstlichen Strumpf' (p.32) in the sense of 'requiring skill to make'; 'Halbstieg' (p.35) or 'halb Stieg' (p.44), 'half a score'. The official epistolary style of the time is imitated in Hauke's application to enclose the *Vorland*, complete with 'insonders' and 'höchstderselben' (p.74).

Nothing is left abstract if Storm can make it concrete. Spring is 'als endlich die Stachelbeeren in ihrem Garten wieder blühten'

(p.10). Hauke well out on the beach lies 'zwischen Strandnelken
und dem duftenden Seewermut' (p.18). Tede Haien deep in
thought 'begann wieder auf und ab zu gehen und spritzte dabei
die schwarze Tabaksjauche von sich' (p.23). Occasionally Storm
uses a pithy saying or local turn of phrase such as 'Dann...soll er
sich den Mund wischen...' (p.38): he will be rejected; or 'so
breit, wie Lawrenz sein Kind nicht lang war' (pp.88f.), probably
referring to Laurentius Damm, a citizen of Hamburg around
1600, whose son was 2m 80cm tall at his confirmation. 'Das war
ein Wurf, sagte Zacharies und warf sein Weib aus der Luke!'
(p.41) shows down-to-earth humour. The sober style is lightened
by such interpolations and by the use of metaphors, especially
for the sea as a wild beast: 'die Wasser beißen heute in den
Deich' (p.12).

Symbolism — always arising from the plot, not indulged in
for its own sake — extends into the smallest details, such as the
deichgräflich armchair, which Hauke is not seen to sit in until he
broaches the plan of the new dyke; then he grips its arms with
'characteristic tenacity' (*33*, p.782). He occupies it again after
winning the fight to get the new sea-wall accepted; when beset by
worries about the dyke he flings himself into it but gets up again
as if 'uncertain of his tenancy' (*33*, p.782). Symbolic description
is found at the completion of the new dyke when the rider
dominates and contrasts with the workers on foot: 'seine hagere
Gestalt auf dem feurigen Schimmel tauchte bald hier, bald dort
aus den schwarzen Menschenmassen empor...' (p.104). The
scene anticipates his pride when he hears the name 'Hauke-
Haien-Koog' and sees himself head and shoulders above all the
Friesians (p.110).

The treatment of nature is atmospheric: 'wüste Dämmerung'
(p.4), 'die heulenden Böen' (p.5), 'der unabsehbare Strand'
(p.15). Occasionally Storm seems to go too far, as when a scene
under the ash tree concludes 'Stille lag über der ungeheueren
Ebene' (p.51): a vastness perhaps more in the human breast than
in the thin strip of Friesian *Marsch*! Conversely, an idyll is also
possible:

der Wind hatte sich gelegt; in anmutigem Fluge schwebten

> Möwen und Avosetten über Land und Wasser hin und wider...aus den weißen Morgennebeln, welche die weite Marsch bedeckten, stieg allmählich ein goldner Herbsttag und beleuchtete das neue Werk der Menschenhände (pp.108f.).

But in general colour is muted. Storm compared his home region thus with the beauties of the bay at Flensburg: 'Hier haben wir nur den großen Wiesenteppich unserer Marschen und die graue Nordseeküste' (to Emil Kuh, 14 May 1875, *11*, II, p.107). Yet there is much loving, careful observation:

> Aus den gefrorenen Gräben, welche allmählich überschritten wurden, funkelte durch die scharfen Schilfspitzen der bleiche Schein der Nachmittagssonne; es fror mächtig... (p.41).

Any version of this in one's own words is unevocative, unexpressive or simply longer than Storm's. Correctly observed detail like the tips of the frozen-in reeds passes imperceptibly into concisely expressed atmosphere: the sun so low as to shine through these tips encapsulates the late afternoon in winter, and is summed up in Storm's powerful word for the degree of frost. Choice of words, sentence-rhythm, alliteration, all play their part in producing a telling vignette.

Or take Hauke and Elke walking home from the dance:

> ein leichter Ostwind wehte und brachte strenge Kälte; die beiden aber gingen, ohne viel Tücher und Umhang, dahin, als sei es plötzlich Frühling worden (pp.48f.).

Most people know how inner experience can make one impervious to outer cold. Storm links this with a theme of the seasons: human warmth makes spring, no weather can stop it. 'Gingen...dahin' suggests insouciance, as if it would only be by chance that their steps actually took them homeward. 'Ohne viel Tücher und Umhang' expresses their failure to wrap up warmly but also hints that warm clothing would have been a complication and hindrance to something very simple in them. 'Brachte strenge Kälte' introduces a harsh, insistent, repetitive rhythm which is broken almost into a waltz time with 'ohne viel Tücher und Umhang, dahin'. The microstructures of the text are often worth examining. In the paragraph beginning 'Dergleichen wiederholte sich an manchem Abend' (p.34), the second, long sentence describing how Hauke gets the negligent rapped over the knuckles is exactly corresponded to by the third describing how Ole spreads the idea that the Haiens are responsible for the trouble; and after these long, abstract formations the earthy words of the neutral or benevolent onlookers form a lighter conclusion.

We are dealing with people whose taciturnity is a well-known local characteristic. A speech of some fourteen lines can suffice for the outpourings of a man's whole heart, the teacher ironically notes (p.54). Storm is at his best when tracing dialogues in which there is more between the lines than actually said, for instance the touching scene in which Elke at last says aloud that Wienke is mentally retarded and Hauke admits to sentimental feelings about the child, freeing Elke from an idea that she herself is somehow at fault (pp.117f.). Masterly use is made of *erlebte Rede*, the procedure which presents thoughts of characters directly as if in their own words, yet in the third person, giving greater identification with the character than conventional reported speech. Thus we have the transition from statements of fact to Hauke's inmost thoughts when he goes for the job at old Volkerts' and determines to have a look at Elke:

> Er kannte sie freilich...doch hatte er noch kaum ein Wort mit ihr gesprochen; nun, wenn er zu dem alten Tede Volkerts ging, wollte er sie doch besser darauf ansehen, was es mit dem Mädchen auf sich habe. Und gleich jetzt wollte er gehen... (p.24).

Occasionally this allows irony, as when Hauke cannot decide whether to join Elke on her walk to the dance at the inn, finally leaving the farm 'als die Gefahr, sie einzuholen, vorüber war' (p.46). In Hauke's final ride, we see things from his viewpoint:

only what he can make out in the gale. The true setting is not the outside world, but his mental landscape. What he does not know — has he crushed Claus? — we do not know. Incident is conveyed as sense-impression: he *feels* the dyke crumbling beneath him (*32*, pp.66f.).

13. Reception

Early reviews of the story suggest some fruitful approaches: they concentrate on the Faustian hero and his pathological traits — whose depiction was much admired —, the question of novel or *Novelle*, the justification for the complex frame, the work's humanistic lessons, the treatment of the eerie and supernatural elements (generally recognised as masterly, but one reviewer found them dispensable: *40*, p.71). But none of this helped the work to capture wide attention. The Wilhelminian public was unreceptive to a work of an unfashionable ethos with its hidden criticism of the era. The eerie elements of the story, a precursor of the early twentieth-century vogue for the grotesque and supernatural, were also insufficient to popularise it. But from 1919 when copyright in Storm's work expired, new editions appeared and the text became much more widely known. In the 1920s it was frequently a set text in German schools — and still is; an opinion poll had it as 'die bekannteste und meistgelesene deutschsprachige Novelle' (*14*, p.207).

Very soon after the first publication, collections of folk-tales started to appear in which, with or without reference to Storm, the story of the white horse rider is treated as a local one, from Eiderstedt. Heinrich Momsen published an interesting version with authentic-sounding differences from Storm's in 1890 (*24*, pp.37-44). But there is no proof yet that the story was in fact being told locally before Storm wrote it down; it was Storm who set off its acceptance as a real piece of the Schleswig-Holstein heritage (*14*, p.213). In line with this naturalisation process are the naming of a new polder completed in 1961 'Hauke-Haien-Koog', which however had nothing to do with the setting of the story (*24*, pp.11-17); and the local popularity of the invented forename Hauke (*14*, p.214). Perhaps today's Friesians have accepted Storm's pleasing legend as the way they would like to see the past of their landscape, rather than facing the historical fact that they had little to do with the improvement of the dykes (*24*, p.115).

After about 1900 Storm became one of the favourites of a *Heimatkunstbewegung* which stressed conservative and closed aspects of rural life but could not grasp Storm's social and metaphysical critiques. As the sentimentalisation of the German countryside is part of the nationalist ideology of blood and soil, it is not surprising that Storm was harnessed for its purposes too. His scenes, style and characters were claimed as specifically German; his conservatism, emphasis on rural society and tendency to idyll were interpreted by reactionary chauvinism as opposition to anything modern or international. Storm's

> 'Gegenwartsbedeutung...liegt in der Heimatliebe und Heimattreue, in der seine Persönlichkeit wurzelt;...in der deutschnationalen Gesinnung, von der seine Dichtung erfüllt ist;...in den Kräften tapferer, aufrechter Mannhaftigkeit, die...den Pulsschlag seines Wesens ausmachen. Er selbst schon hat mit dem trotzigen Selbstbewußtsein, das seinem Stamme eigen ist, um die gerechte Anerkennung für diesen Teil seines Seins und Schaffens gekämpft.'[10]

Nationalists after 1919 found certain of Storm's outpourings useful to their purpose. He appeals to German ideals in the hope of achieving peace and democracy in Schleswig; they posit that he wished for a greater, stronger *Reich* to the exclusion of all else.

Around 1900 critics also start noting, with vague ethnology, something Nordic about Hauke Haien. Appreciations of his decisiveness and hardness use a vocabulary which sounds proto-Hitlerian: the dominant character, his selfishness and greed forgotten, is celebrated as one of the heroes of the age. A variation on the Nordic theme is the tendency to idealise the Friesian. Storm rarely describes figures in his works as

[10] Friedrich Düsel, in the volume edited by him: *Gedenkbuch zu des Dichters hundertstem Geburtstag* (Brunswick, 1916), pp.8f., quoted in *37*, p.2.

specifically Friesian, and they are disparate types: he had no
racial or tribal ideal. But critics found one, and stylised this ideal
Friesian into an ideal leader — disregarding the fact that the
obstructive mass must be equally Friesian! The misuse of the
text in schools as a way of introducing the inland child to the
people and landscape of the northern seaboard also encouraged
some nonsense about Friesian types (*24*, pp.100-03).

During the First World War some critics admit Hauke's moral
guilt but see it as an inevitable part of the march of progress.
Only ambition and guilt get the dyke built. The leader onward is
not subject to the usual ethical norms, but is a quasi-Nietzschean
amoral superman. Didactic interpretations of the twenties tend
to put the work at the service of the fashions and ideologies of
the era, with its demand for a strong leader to rescue weak
Germany from its plight after the Versailles 'Diktat', rather than
to examine Storm's own intention and achievements. We find
descriptions of Hauke as 'Führer', a 'nordischer Rassenmensch'
with a right to impose himself on the 'Masse, die zu führen
ist'.[11] All writing on the story under Hitler then sees Hauke as an
example of the *Führerprinzip* at work, of the biologically
predestined emergence of the superior individual from the racial
mass, of the ineffable fascination of the destined leader.

The story was brought forcefully to public attention in 1934
by a film by Curt Oertel. 'Geschlossen wurden die Schulklassen
in die Kinos geführt und erlebten dort den einsamen, ebenso
opferwilligen wie eisenharten Führer, der sich im Stil Adolf
Hitlers mit demagogischer Rhetorik an sein Volk wendet' (*19*,
p.112). The struggle with the backward elements of the
community parallels Hitler's struggle for power. The idiot child
is omitted as not befitting a member of the Master Race — or
because the handicapped are poor box office? Technically the
film was interesting for its realistic exterior shots and use of
authentic settings and props. A television film screened in 1981
with John Philipp Law playing the hero in western cowboy style
and Gert Froebe as old Volkerts distorts plot and character and

[11] Thus in Eilhard Erich Pauls, 'Die Tragik des Schimmelreiters', *Volk und
Rasse* 2 (1927), Heft 2, Beilage Volk und Wort, 126-130, quoted in *19*, p.112.

is even more superficial than the 1934 film.

After 1945 scholars, starting with an American, Walter Silz, started trying to rescue Storm from distortions of his intentions and put the interpretation on the basis of the text seen in the context of its own era. At the same time local historians did much work on the sources and topographical reality of the story — an activity not always free from an unhealthy ethnic pride (the same danger of a return to *Heimatkunst* attitudes is present in fresh attention given to local roots in the ecologically-minded eighties). Many writers on Storm still have Nordic and pseudo-Friesian ideals in mind. 'Die Gestalt des Schimmelreiters ist ein Sinnbild der ganzen friesischen Meereslandschaft und ihres Volkstums, der ewigen Unruhe, des Kampfwillens, der Schöpferkraft des nordischen Menschen' (*34*, p.108). His willpower and Elke's are seen as illuminating a *Stamm* characteristic. Meanwhile a vogue of *Existenzphilosophie* brought about much talk of the timeless and elemental aspects of Storm, of a vague riddle of existence, a self-proclamation arising from the depths of artistic sensitivity, and suchlike. Later, starting in East Germany with Goldammer and Böttger, and continuing in the west with Hermand and Vinçon, attention was drawn more to the social aspects of Storm's work.

14. Four Views of the Story

Der Schimmelreiter has lent itself to diverse, sometimes diametrically opposed, interpretations. Storm brings in a set of contradictions, dichotomies and ambiguities that allow no clear resolution, questions with no single answer. Our assessment of Hauke — and hence of his conflict with those around him, and of the theme of the whole *Novelle* — is a matter of critical strife: is he a hero or a villain, idealistic or money-grubbing, governed by reason or passion? To Ellis it is wrong to look for a 'balanced' judgment on him, as Storm has written 'two contradictory and irresolvable views of Hauke into his story' (*18*, p.163): Christlike or in league with the devil, killing Trin' Jans's cat but saving the dog. These two views arise from the 'legend' status of the story and have at least as much to do with 'different perspectives on the ideas for which he stands' (p.163) taken by different tellers of the legend as with any 'real' Hauke.

If we disregard interpretations in the spirit of Nazism or *Blut und Boden* ideology, we find four main approaches to the story, perhaps best summed up in the contributions of Barz, Martini, Hermand and M. Peischl: respectively the autobiographical, the existential, the socio-economic and the psychoanalytical. The simplest is the autobiographical. Barz points out that Hauke has much of Storm. The reproach of having botched a job while weak and tired is one Storm makes to himself regarding the imperfections of *Ein Bekenntnis*. Storm's cancer showed itself in alternations of short periods of energy and long periods of apathy which meant that work on *Der Schimmelreiter* proceeded in fits and starts; Haien too shows occasional energy and lives quietly for long periods in between. The boy with talent, laughed at at first, then successful but still alone, fighting for recognition, consoling himself with the thought that his work will survive him and prove him to have been a great man in his field, is Storm, if we look behind his carefully nurtured friendships with a few kindred spirits: none of his schoolmates was close to him. The dyke is a product of genius: a transposition of Storm's poetic work, which he could scarcely expect the Friesians to appreciate, into practical terms.

Hauke is obsessed by the jealousy, real or imagined, of his fellow-villagers who begrudge him his office; Storm spoilt his seventieth birthday celebrations by a tirade against the dead Geibel, who, he felt, had usurped the attention due to him as a poet. Storm took a rigid view of his social position and had no social dealings with the lower class; Hauke sees his workers only as a mass. Hauke's father laughs at his plans; Storm too had an intelligent father, who never read his literary works. Tede Haien helps Hauke to grow richer; Johann Storm long supported Theodor financially. Hauke's mother is absent; Storm's mother a shadowy figure. Elke, the kindred spirit but addressed without erotic warmth, is an ideal wife as envisaged by Storm when he wanted Constanze to educate herself to his level, but the marriage is flawed by Wienke as Storm's life was overshadowed by Hans's problems (*14*, pp.195-202). Thus much of the stuff of the story is a transposition of Storm's own life. However, the autobiographical approach can at best show, in part speculatively, whence the author had certain components of his work; it cannot explain the artistic result of his treatment of them.

Martini, in the spirit of post-1945 existentialism, believes that in *Der Schimmelreiter* Storm at last left behind 'die bürgerlichen Sicherungen' (*30*, p.662) to show tragically 'die Ausgesetztheit des Menschen im radikalen Widerspruch' (p.664). The story has a harmony of opposites: psychological probability and yet unfathomable, eerie elements; tragedy from within and outside the character; Hauke as 'sozialer Emporkömmling und seelischer Aristokrat' (*30*, p.662); guilt, fate, chance as motive forces. 'Ein psychologisches Geschick, sozial begründet, durch Volksnatur und Umwelt determiniert, geht in die Traumwirklichkeit des Magisch-Gespenstischen über, die sich in Gerücht und Sage spiegelt. Volkstypus und Landschaft, das Elementare, Ungebändigte eines eigensinnig harten Charakters, Wille und Getriebenheit, Leidenschaft und Verhängnis bilden das Ganze

eines vielschichtigen Schicksals' (*30*, p.662; note that much of
the vocabulary is that of the Hitler era, shorn of the overtly
political elements). Hauke, a heightened version of the
impassioned, single-minded characters frequent in Storm's late
work, represents a new generation breaking apart the old and
outworn until he challenges fate too far. Perhaps his
immoderacy is a moral failing; but his guilt is not a moral one,
rather 'eine Existenzschuld, die im Unbedingten des Willens
liegt, den zwar das objektive Werk rechtfertigt, der aber im
subjektiv Ichhaften vermessen wird' (*30*, p.663).

Hauke fights to secure the land against the elements and thus
allows the irruption of the sea; his wish to tame the elements
puts him at their mercy. The cool calculator becomes an
obsessed dreamer. From insignificance he rises to leadership,
but in so doing becomes dependent on those he has left behind
and despises. His passion for deeds is a sign of a weakness he
feels as *Deichgraf* through his wife and as father of a backward
child. He wants order and unleashes chaos. He wants to leave a
lasting work; his family is doomed to ruin. He owes half his life
to Elke and pulls her down with him. Superstition enmeshes his
free intellect. Trying to be the master he becomes the victim of
his work. In serving the community he uses force against it; duty
to the whole makes him lonely. When he moderates and
compromises, this too turns against him and becomes guilt.
Perdition and right are always mingled. Even after death he is
chained to his work; only as a frightening, unredeemed ghost
does he have the immortality he craved. However great man's
struggle, however heroic his ambition, however hard he works
for progress, he is still unprotected when he faces the paradoxes
of fate.

Hermand, one of the pioneers of a shift in German studies in
the sixties towards more social or socialist orientation, gives a
very different interpretation of Hauke's single-mindedness: he is
not just a typical late Storm hero, but a figure of Storm's era,
one of the hard and uncompromising men who are the literary
echo of the *Gründerzeit*, like Conrad Ferdinand Meyer's
protagonists or Nietzsche's Zarathustra. The age replaces
psychological relativism, balance and moderation by 'eine

Machtideologie, die nur den Weg nach vorne kennt' (*22*, p.256). The hero is a great individual, standing alone, practically without human converse, admired, not analysed. The sea is a suitable backdrop for him. He educates himself to hardness and courage, he carries around inner resentments. A great task, an aim before his eyes, seems to him the suitable fulfilment of his life. He reaches the primary aim of becoming *Deichgraf* through Elke's love, but for the hero of the imperial age this is not good enough: he must owe his greatness only to himself. He single-mindedly pursues the building of the dyke, he sees the villagers as dogs and seems to want to whip them (p.67). Everyone is harnessed before the chariot of his fame; 'der Wille zur Verewigung der eigenen Persönlichkeit durch eine alles überragende Leistung' (*22*, p.259) replaces reason.

When he buys the horse he grows further away from the mass of people. As in old legends the supernatural seems to be at his service: Faust has found his Mephisto. He becomes a personified natural force, a 'Dämon der Küste' (*22*, p.260). Psychological interpretation is left behind: only his activity and creativity count. Nothing, not the dull child, not the inertia of the masses, can stop him. Such a life must end tragically and dramatically. His end is compared with that of Christ and Socrates, not with religious intention, but to show his importance. The schoolmaster, Hermand claims, might agree with Nietzsche: 'Die schrecklichen Energien — das, was man das Böse nennt — sind die zyklopischen Architekten und Wegebauer der Humanität.'[12]

But another level of narrative intention casts doubt on any tendency to admire Hauke. Storm has after all been writing since long before 1870, and his long-held liberal-conservative attitudes have not crumbled in the new historical situation. He does not use grandiose abstract scenery like Meyer, but a well-defined locality; the sea is not only symbolic but real; we find specialised or local words that other authors would have avoided in order to retain classical purity. The supernatural is not a literary cipher for superhuman greatness, but a part of the local

---

[12] Nietzsche, *Werke* (Leipzig, 1899ff.), II, p.231, quoted in *22*, p.261.

character in the home of second sight. Hauke's marriage is not just a way to power, but an example of the ways of the taciturn Friesians. He himself is neither noble genius nor black villain, but a man with a talent that will remain frustrated if he does not create room to exercise it. This visionary does his sums: he is both Nietzschean superman and enlightenment progressive; he works for money, a very real spur in those years, but one that was thought unworthy of a poetic hero. He is not conceived of as *Jenseits von Gut und Böse*, to use Nietzschean terms; greatness does not excuse his misdeeds; his end seems a punishment. 'Hier wird nicht nur Mythisches beschworen, sondern zugleich moralisch abgewogen und geurteilt' (*22*, p.267). Yet the achievement remains. So the urge to power and the moral conscience are kept in an unresolved dialectical relationship. Similarly many men like Storm rejected Bismarck's way to German unity, but had to admit that the country made progress in the following years. Hermand thus believes, in the spirit of the era of *littérature engagée*, that a specific problem of Storm's day is at the heart of the work.

In the last interpretation, using Jungian psychology and the theory of the mythical hero, Storm's 'life-long struggle with Christianity, his indifference to the "große Welt" of history, politics and scientific progess, his fatalistic attitude toward life, his obsession with death and the question of the after-life, his interest in the occult and the superstitions and legendry of his Frisian world' show 'characteristics that betray a soul especially sensitive to the pagan Germanic spirit of his forebears' (*31*, p.113). The story is 'the tale of a hero, his "dragon" fight and acquisition of a "treasure" (...the construction of a dyke to conquer the treacherous North Sea and to reclaim usable land), the assistance he receives from an animal (a mysterious white horse), an apocalyptic flood, the hero's sacrifice of self to atone for the sin of hubris, and his ultimate rebirth as a supernatural being, a Wotan-like ghost rider' (*31*, p.112); 'the struggle of the heroic male against the archetypal Great Mother and his self-willed demise as a result of his inability to extricate himself from his own destructive attachment to her...an attempt of the pagan Germanic soul to progress spiritually and intellectually and to rescue itself from the grip of the all-devouring, undifferentiated feminine principle, i.e. the chaotic unconscious' (*31*, pp.114f.) which, however, maintains 'validity and power...throughout the entire narrative' (*31*, p.115).

Hauke has a one-sided masculine nature, wants to develop his conscious intellect and suppress 'that side of his own nature whose strength he subconsciously recognizes and equates with the raging sea' (*31*, p.116). Trin' Jans's cat links him with a negative anima figure. Elke can add no feminine dimension to his being, she is rather an anima-sister or helpmate. The *Eisboseln* is the traditional test by which the hero wins his predecessor's daughter and assumes rule himself. In the second half, having planned the dyke on his own, Hauke needs the mysterious horse to enable its actual construction. The horse is masculine — unlike his previous gelding — and active, but deeper down feminine, having a special relationship to the Great Mother, able to call 'Hauke's dormant intuitive life, his anima' (*31*, p.121) into action; when he rides it, reason barely controls his instinctive unconscious life. Later illness weakens his willpower, he adopts a passive self-defeating attitude: 'a victory of internal sea serpents of the subconscious allied with that dragon represented by the sea which he defeated with his dike' (*31*, p.123). He retreats from the conscious and social activity into the unconscious. He is reluctant to ride the horse, to 'call upon his potentially creative subconscious' (*31*, p.123): a 'mythical hero who has lost favour with the gods' (ibid.).

The interested reader should consult Peischl's essay for him or herself. To me the interpretation is vague, ambiguous and self-contradictory and merely replaces one set of problems by another; there are no doubt archetypes whose appearance in literary works strikes a chord in the reader, but references to the Germanic soul seem unlikely to help in elucidating them.

Conclusion

All these interpretations have some justification. Indeed the combination of various elements in the work is a component of classic greatness, and the story aims to create a myth of a modern tragic hero, no less. Storm's narrative skills would be hollow if the story did not confront the reader with questions of basic human values. We are called on to reflect on man's treatment of nature and fellow man, and on the ways in which nature and fellow men will have their revenge if maltreated. At the end of *Faust* Part II, Goethe, an author revered by Storm, has the hero conceiving and executing plans of land reclamation intended to provide the space for a prosperous life for many people, and redolent of the same spirit of enterprise which was to flourish in post-1871 Germany. If Faust had hitherto been egocentric and subject to the dominion of Mephistopheles, the Luciferian figure, he now challenges the elements for the common good and concludes:

> Nur der verdient sich Freiheit wie das Leben,
> Der täglich sie erobern muß.
> Und so verbringt, umrungen von Gefahr,
> Hier Kindheit, Mann und Greis sein tüchtig Jahr.
> Solch ein Gewimmel möcht' ich sehn,
> Auf freiem Grund mit freiem Volke stehn.
> Zum Augenblicke dürft ich sagen:
> Verweile doch, du bist so schön!
> Es kann die Spur von meinen Erdetagen
> Nicht in Äonen untergehn.

The desire to keep the passing moment is what Mephisto has been waiting for to enforce the bargain by which he can claim Faust's soul: but Faust's strivings have saved him and he is

Conclusion

received into Heaven. Hauke's end is the opposite. Proud of his own work, he saves it, thus possibly becoming guilty of the loss of the old polder, of which he is accused (p.140). The lights go out. The bodies are taken by the sea, claimed as satisfaction for Hauke's hubris. The forces of nature take their revenge on the pride of the individual.

The ever-present threat of the sea as the force of chaos can only be kept back in the long run by a concerted effort of the community combined with the innovative vision of a leader. All human achievements are threatened by primordial forces; man must do all he can to order his world, by way of rational calculation, intuitive reaction, and the order of society and family. Here Hauke's relationships with society and family are underdeveloped. Loneliness, silence, ambition largely replace communication, trust, mutual care, the warmth of human company. The manifold cracks in the structure of society — a social phenomenon relevant to the time of writing — allow the natural catastrophe at the end by hindering proper preventative action beforehand. 'Nicht den Triumph der Naturgewalt über Menschenwerk schildert die Novelle, sondern das Scheitern sozialer Integration' (*19*, p.95). Old and new, collective and individual fail to work together; the natural disaster is their punishment. Rogers sees the ending as symbolic: 'He is the new dyke, the community is the old' (*32*, p.192). Their common safety depends on how they are joined. Hauke is too individualistic, rigid and authoritarian, and rejects the demand for a sacrifice: 'that he cement the join by throwing *himself*, his own living personality, into it' (*32*, p.193). When the crisis arises he endangers the community, he refuses to let himself be destroyed, so the breach between him and the community is opened up and he perishes in it.

Storm examines a mentality still familiar a hundred years later: a tendency to technocracy, the belief that all problems can be solved by a scientific theory and its application in technical practice; a utilitarian and egoistic way of thinking which, starting with a new and useful idea, makes and loses fortunes as it presses ahead with schemes to make money out of technical and scientific advance (silicon chips, home computers) or to

improve the material quality of life in the short term, neglecting
the quality of human interrelations and the long-term integrity
of the environment. Against such two-dimensional attitudes we
should put an awareness of deeper forces which express
themselves in vague and shifting ways, yet urgently, in the
paranormal and mythical. The eerie is a necessary reminder to us
that there is a non-technical reality. The family too embodies
alternative values. Hauke's way of thinking is a masculine one;
he does not let himself be swayed by Elke's views in deciding on
the project meant to prove his independence of her. Women no
more participate in entrepreneurial activity today than in the late
nineteenth or the mid-eighteenth centuries, though social dis-
crimination against them is less. If allowed a voice, they would
perhaps humanise the masculine competitive society.

Precisely at a time of material progress and the freedom to
make a profit under a democratic capitalist society, each person
needs to ask for him or herself what the ethical bases of action
are. No binding moral system, no force of social convention, no
state intervention will prevent brutal arrogance, egoism and
greed. No inherent natural magic will ensure that all progress
benefits all of mankind. The community has to ensure this. In
the story, this does not happen; the prevailing lethargy, small-
mindedness and hostility of the village community bear their
share of responsibility for the social catastrophe. The people
have no will to integrate the exceptional individual. By failing to
make Hauke one of them they miss the chance to check his
egoism and hubris whilst making his talent and energy work for
them. They isolate Hauke with their superstitiousness and
bigotry, which give a focus to the workings of all too human
envy and meanness. Comparison with Brecht's *Leben des Galilei*
shows this clearly. There, an alliance of feudalism and religious
obscurantism ensures that technical progress remains isolated
from social progress, which however will in the end sweep away
feudalism — and then capitalism — and improve human nature.
Here, feudalism is given no chance and capitalism works
without exploitation, yet obscurantism is able to put obstacles in
the way of the amelioration of mankind. Storm defends
constant social structures, gradual organic change, power based

on competence, and a property-owning society whose inequalities are modified by paternalistic benevolence; but as man is imperfect and nature hostile, an ideal society is not in sight.

Superstition is castigated — and we who live in an age when astrology is popular should not think this irrelevent to ourselves. But awareness of the supernatural throws up some insights which rational thought cannot evade — here the need for a living sacrifice to the dyke. The life of the rational improver is thus by definition tragic, he is bound to come into conflict with paranormal forces just as valid as his own strivings. Hauke's self-sacrifice after he refused to allow the sacrifice of a dog can be seen as an atonement or surrender to the myth-making powers of the common people who with one voice demand a living sacrifice to make the dyke hold. There is also a sense in which Hauke fails because after fighting the idea of the need for a sacrifice — whether we see this idea as valid metaphysical thought, or an image hinting at a truth which cannot be directly and exactly expressed, or as mere superstition — he is at the end forced to offer the sacrifice: a negation of all he has stood for.

The outcome of an individual's struggle is also necessarily tragic because of biological decadence. But even more important is the pessimistic idea that one's best is never good enough. To Storm, in 1880, not 'die eigene Schuld allein' makes a story of failure into tragedy, but 'Der vergebliche Kampf gegen das, was durch die Schuld oder auch nur die Begrenzung, die Unzulänglichkeit des Ganzen, der Menschheit, von der der (wie man sich ausdrückt) Held ein Teil ist, der sich nicht abzulösen vermag, und sein oder seines eigentlichen Lebens herbei-geführter Untergang scheint mir das Allertragischste' (*Was der Tag gibt*, quoted *4*, I, p.54). Hauke, weak from illness, lets himself be persuaded that a superficial repair will save the dykes; in a quite classical manner, this small flaw, this understandable lapse from his own high standards, unleashes the tragedy. In *Ein Bekenntnis* Storm expressed this with rather intrusive tragic irony: a doctor gives up hope for his wife's life, is so distraught that, in contrast to his usual conscientiousness, he does not read the latest medical journal, gives her a fatal overdose to save her suffering, and afterwards discovers in the unread journal a report of a new operation which could have saved her.

Der Schimmelreiter does not have the weaknesses of *Ein Bekenntnis*. Silz regards it as Storm's masterpiece: leaving behind the pathetic, the accidental, the merely harrowing, he achieves tragedy — a great and formidable hero concisely but memorably described, a primal contest, a complex view of guilt and fate. Storm shows the configuration of progressive and regressive forces in humankind, the clashes of individual and collective, man and nature. The concrete, circumscribed community is a model for general truths; its simplicity helps to bring them out starkly. In the conflict of the great individual with his work for progress, order and reason on the one hand, and the forces of reaction, chaos, superstition and dogma on the other, the balance of right and wrong is a shifting one. Storm prefers the progressive but cannot deny some truth in the regressive. Progress exacts a high price. The dyke holds; but there is a disastrous flood, Hauke's family is exterminated and his memory distorted. Optimism about technical progress is balanced by pessimism about the individual fate (*20*, p.450) and about social progress. Storm seems not to think it worthwhile to meditate on the ideal state: he shows all the forces that militate against it and is pessimistic. Are we pessimistic or optimistic? Can a reading of this story, despite Storm's own views, give us grounds for optimism, or at least tools to help avoid the worst outcome of social processes?

Select Bibliography

A. EDITIONS

1. Theodor Storm, *Der Schimmelreiter*: Novelle. Mit einem Nachwort von Wolfgang Heybey, Reclams Universal-Bibliothek (Stuttgart: Reclam, 1963).
2. Theodor Storm, *Der Schimmelreiter*, ed. with an introduction and notes by E.H. Burrough (London: Harrap, 1953; reprinted Walton-on-Thames: Nelson, 1986).
3. Theodor Storm, *Sylter Novelle: Skizze; Der Schimmelreiter*, ed. Karl Ernst Laage (Heide: Boyens, 1970), with reproductions of old documents and maps and *Der gespenstige Reiter* after the oldest known source.
4. The best collected edition of Storm's works today: Theodor Storm, *Sämtliche Werke*, 4 vols, ed. Peter Goldammer (Berlin and Weimar: Aufbau, 1956, 6th ed., 1986). Another version of the introduction to this edition, published separately with good illustrations: Peter Goldammer, *Theodor Storm: Eine Einführung in Leben und Werk* (Leipzig: Reclam, 1968).
5. Theodor Storm, *Der Schimmelreiter*, ed. Margaret L. Mare, with English vocabulary (London: Methuen, 1957, new ed. 1973).

B. STORM'S LETTERS:

6. Theodor Storm — Paul Heyse, *Briefwechsel*, ed. Clifford Albrecht Bernd, 3 vols (Berlin: E. Schmidt, 1969-74).
7. *Der Briefwechsel zwischen Theodor Storm und Gottfried Keller*, ed. Peter Goldammer (Berlin: Aufbau, 1960).
8. *Theodor Storms Briefwechsel mit Theodor Mommsen*, ed. Hans-Erich Teitge (Weimar: Böhlau, 1966).
9. Theodor Storm — Wilhelm Petersen, *Briefwechsel*, ed. Brian Coghlan (Berlin: E. Schmidt, 1984).
10. Theodor Storm — Erich Schmidt, *Briefwechsel*, ed. Karl Ernst Laage, 2 vols (Berlin: E. Schmidt, 1972-76).
11. Theodor Storm, *Briefe*, ed. Peter Goldammer, 2 vols (Berlin: Aufbau, 1972). A selection.

C. SECONDARY WORKS (chosen not mainly for their importance or influence in Storm scholarship, but for their usefulness to me and their potential usefulness to the reader):

12. Arthur Tilo Alt, *Theodor Storm* (New York: Twayne, 1973).

13. David Artiss, 'Bird Motif and Myth in Theodor Storm's *Schimmelreiter*', *Seminar* 4 (1968), 1-16.

14. Paul Barz, *Der wahre Schimmelreiter* (Hamburg: Kabel, 1982). In popularising style; much on North Friesian history and reality as related to the story.

15. Fritz Böttger, *Theodor Storm in seiner Zeit* (Berlin: Verlag der Nation, 1959). Read with care because of over-keenness to prove Storm's modernity and radicalism.

16. Annemarie Burchard, 'Theodor Storms "Schimmelreiter": Ein Mythos im Werden', *Antaios* 2 (1960-61), 456-69.

17. Günther Ebersold, *Politik und Gesellschaftskritik in den Novellen Theodor Storms* (Frankfurt: Lang, 1981).

18. John M. Ellis, *Narration in the German Novelle* (Cambridge: University Press, 1974).

19. Winfried Freund, *Theodor Storm: Der Schimmelreiter: Glanz und Elend des Bürgers* (Paderborn: Schöningh, 1984). The fullest up-to-date study, with maps and pictures; too concerned to play down the paranormal.

20. Wolfgang Frühwald, 'Hauke Haien, der Rechner...', in J. Brummack et al. (eds): *Literaturwissenschaft und Geistesgeschichte*: Festschrift R. Brinkmann (Tübingen: Niemeyer, 1981), pp.438-57. Interesting, but the interpretation seems self-contradictory.

21. Thomas Heine, '*Der Schimmelreiter*. An Analysis of the Narrative Structure', *German Quarterly* 55 (1982), 554-64.

22. Jost Hermand, 'Hauke Haien. Kritik oder Ideal des gründerzeitlichen Übermenschen?' in his *Von Mainz nach Weimar* (Stuttgart: Metzler, 1969), pp.250-68.

23. Wolfgang Heybey, 'Theodor Storm. *Der Schimmelreiter*', in *Lehrpraktische Analysen*, Folge 29 (Stuttgart, Reclam, 1969), pp.3-19.

24. Reimer May Holander, *Theodor Storm: Der Schimmelreiter: Kommentar und Dokumentation* (Frankfurt/Main: Ullstein 1976).

25. Karl Ernst Laage, 'Der ursprüngliche Schluß der Stormschen Schimmelreiter-Novelle', *Euphorion* 73 (1979), 451-57.

26. Ilse Langer, 'Volksaberglauben und paranormales Geschehen in einigen Szenen des "Schimmelreiters"', *Schriften der Theodor-Storm-Gesellschaft* 24 (1975), 90-97.

27. Gotthard Lerchner und Hans-Georg Werner, 'Probleme der semantischen Analyse eines poetischen Textes...', *Weimarer Beiträge* 21 (1975), Heft 10, 100-136.

28. William F. Mainland, 'Theodor Storm', in *German Men of Letters: Twelve Literary Essays*, ed. Alex Natan (London: O. Wolff, 1961), 147-68. Short, but outdated and fallible introduction to Storm in English.

29. Margaret Mare, *Theodor Storm and his World* (Cambridge: Cambridge Aids to Learning, 1976). Unanalytical and oddly presented, but the fullest life of Storm in English.
30. Fritz Martini, *Deutsche Literatur im bürgerlichen Realismus, 1848-1898* (Stuttgart: Metzler, 1962), pp.662-64.
31. Margaret T. Peischl, 'The Persistence of the Pagan in Theodor Storm's *Der Schimmelreiter*', *Seminar* 22 (1986), 112-25.
32. Terence John Rogers, *Techniques of Solipsism...* (Cambridge: Modern Humanities Research Association, 1970).
33. Walter Silz, 'Theodor Storm's *Schimmelreiter*', *Publications of the Modern Language Association* 61 (1946), 762-83. Still useful, has some details lacking in more recent essays.
34. Franz Stuckert, *Theodor Storm: Der Dichter in seinem Werk*, 2nd ed. (Tübingen: Niemeyer, 1952). Read with care because of elements of *Blut und Boden* ideology.
35. Martin Swales, *The German Novelle* (Princeton: University Press, 1977). On *Novelle*, not on *Der Schimmelreiter*.
36. Harmut Vinçon, *Theodor Storm*, Rowohlts Monographien (Reinbek: Rowohlt, 1972).
37. ——, *Theodor Storm* (Stuttgart: Metzler, 1973).
38. Alfred D. White, 'Society, Progress and Reaction in *Der Schimmelreiter*', *New German Studies* 12 (1984), 151-73.
39. Lothar Wittmann, 'Theodor Storm: *Der Schimmelreiter*', in Heinrich Gaese et al.: *Deutsche Novellen des 19. Jahrhunderts*, 2nd ed. (Frankfurt/Main: Diesterweg, 1964), pp.50-92. Valuable if one-sided interpretation stressing Hauke's psychology.
40. *Erläuterungen und Dokumente zu Theodor Storm: Der Schimmelreiter*, ed. Hans Wagener, Reclams Universal-Bibliothek (Stuttgart: Reclam, 1976). It has a plan of the localities, factual notes, documents on the work's genesis and reception, historical and literary sources including *Der gespenstige Reiter* after Storm's source, passages from Goethe's *Faust* for comparison, texts on theory of *Novelle* from, before and after Storm's time, and a bibliography.